CHILL

Embrace the Space Between Extremes

Shawn Langwell

ISBN: 978-1-967184-00-2

First paperback edition June 30, 2025

Editing, Cover, and Design by Crissi Langwell / North Coast Stories

Author photo by Stuart Lirette

This book is also available as an eBook.

ShawnLangwell.com

For David O'Connor, Dale Godfrey, and other bold and visionary leaders, mentors, and teachers, past, present, and future who understand the power and value of love, honesty, and compassion to unify people from all walks of life.

Table of Contents

Introduction

A few months ago, I had lunch with a former co-worker and boss. After catching up about family and work, our conversation turned to current events, politics, spirituality, and writing. I mentioned this book and how I was struggling to find the right way to distill my thoughts succinctly without pointing fingers.

Over the next twenty minutes, we discussed several tough topics. Topics that were and are weighing on our minds and, according to recent headlines and articles, also loom heavy on the hearts and minds of many around the world.

Our conversation was like a game of public opinion ping pong, only it wasn't a debate. No need to convince or convert. Just open and honest conversation about what we—individually and collectively, as a culture— might do to make this world better for all.

We talked about women's rights, the polarization and divisiveness between the "liberal left" and "conservative right." About racial inequality, social justice (injustice), and the exorbitantly high cost of living in California. We even touched on religion and politics. All the taboo topics people normally don't discuss over a meal, let alone in public. It was liberating to speak freely without fear of argument or retaliatory vitriol.

Though neither of us had specific solutions for any of the issues we discussed, halfway through our lunch it hit me—I felt butterflies doing backflips in my gut and I knew.

This book isn't about me. It's about us.

What can we, individually and collectively, do better? What tough questions must we ask ourselves? What fears do I need to face? What can I control and what do I need to let go of? What changes am I willing to make to be a kinder human?

What's it About?

This is a relationship book about healing, connection, and acceptance. About bridging the divides that separate us—whether political, religious, spiritual, or cultural—and creating space for our differences without judgment or fear.

It's about learning to take personal responsibility for our thoughts, attitudes, and actions. About ending the blame game. About how we can learn to play in the same sandbox without flinging sand at each other.

You may not agree with everything I share. That's okay—healthy disagreement is part of growth. I do, however, ask that you approach this work with an open mind and a willingness to do better.

This book is for anyone craving a little more kindness and connection. For those who want to be seen, heard, and accepted. It's also for those ready to break cycles of suffering, fear, guilt, and shame.

It is my hope that the stories and insights I share from my middle-class hippie upbringing to now meet you where you are and challenge you to become comfortable with uncertainty. The Unknown. The space between extremes.

That you practice looking objectively at the extremes of any situation, and instead of forming a snap judgement, take a beat to become more curious. To chill.

Try instead to ask deeper introspective questions before pointing a finger. For example:

"What are you trying to say to me?"
"What do you want me to do?"
"Is there another side to this argument?"
"What is this trying to teach me?"

Ultimately, I wrote this book **to heal and bridge the growing divide between us**.

I wrote it because I know we all can do better.

Chapter 1: For Freedom

"For to be free is not merely to cast off ones chains, but to live in a way that respects and enhances the freedom of others."
Nelson Mandela

Life is not black or white.

It's a thousand shades of gray, often found in the valleys between emotionally-loaded, snow-capped peaks and seemingly bottomless pits of sadness or despair. It's the space between the ebb and flow of endless tides. The turbulent tumble of stones worn smooth or turned to sand from years of endless pounding by salty sea or winter stream.

Life is not all or nothing. It just is.

It's a gift meant to be cherished and shared. It is also a process of continuous transformation to be experienced and embraced. It is not to be squandered or wasted on mundane obsessions such as worry, fear, or doubt.

Life is not all about more. Of getting or having so much stuff that we have to pay to store it.

It's also not all about survival, living paycheck to paycheck, incessantly worrying about earning enough money to put food on the table or a roof over our heads.

And yet most of us, if we're honest, focus way too much on these extremes—the black and white, good or bad, left or right, love or hate, heaven or hell, success or failure, rich or poor, old or young, happy or sad.

Such extreme values, attitudes, or beliefs do not define us. Nor are they always good or bad. Quite simply, they are the fringes of a bell curve. The extremes which enable us to fully understand and experience the plethora of human emotion. The inevitable ups and downs, joys and sorrows, struggles and victories, triumphs and tragedies, which comprise the majestic tapestry of our fluid and dynamic lives.

The Problem: We Are Addicted to Extremes

All too often we attach our self-worth and identities to external factors or measures. In the process, we lose sight of who we truly are.

We wear masks or build walls to protect our pride or ego. We avoid being truly vulnerable or authentic because we desperately want to be loved and accepted. Ironically as we do, we block ourselves from the possibility and opportunity to connect. To heal. To love. When we chose to be a victim or play the insidious game of *blame, shame, guilt*, we unconsciously ostracize ourselves from others.

That's a lonely life and it's not healthy.

Conversely, when we righteously preach about "our way or the highway," we only add bricks to towering walls and create an even greater divide between *us* and *them*. We fail to connect. Ultimately, driven by fear, we lock ourselves in our own prison and throw away the key.

Hard Truths

Our white-knuckled grip to what we know and what is comfortable inhibits our ability to fully experience joy and inner peace.

Our stubborn refusal to be more curious and open-minded tethers us to a wall of denial and slams shut the windows to our soul, dark shades drawn tight, further blocking us from the sunlight of the spirit within.

Trust me, I know how lonely such attitudes can be and I wouldn't wish them for anyone.

But there is hope.

For us to know peace and what it means to be truly free (*assuming that we want inner-peace and freedom*), it is imperative that we learn to embrace the space between extremes. That we seek to expand our understanding of personal, mental, physical, and spiritual freedoms *purposefully and intentionally*. That we become *enlightened, awakened*, and *learn to nurture and share the endless gifts we already possess inside*.

Equally important and irrespective of personal spiritual beliefs, we have an obligation to be healthy stewards of our gifts, especially our innate capacity to give and receive love.

As spiritual beings in a physical form, our purpose is simple: to love God *(whatever that means to you)*, ourselves, and others.

It is our responsibility to embrace and not resist our spiritual nature. We do this by honoring our highest self through acts of kindness and compassion to ourselves and others.

The joy we seek comes as a result of practice, not theory or dogma. Of thinking about ourselves less and others a bit more. Of relinquishing our supposed need for certainty and control so we can learn how to embrace the vast unknown.

This is where we experience the mysteries and miracles of life. We discover the boundless potential of life when we take time for quiet reflection, perhaps during a calming seaside stroll, noticing the details like the salty air and diving pelicans.

True freedom is not found in carefully calculated plans and designs, though they can be helpful. It's found when we embrace the unknown and let go of what no longer serves us or others.

Inner peace is found when we stop trying to control everyone and everything in our world; all the illusions we think and believe we need.

To know freedom and create inner peace and happiness, we must learn the art of letting go.

Most of our problems are the result of decisions and choices we have made, usually based on some form of fear. In and of themselves, fear and expressing emotions are not bad. Problems arise when we believe fears that are not real and allow our emotions to control our attitude and outlook upon life.

Also, failing to forgive and choosing to hold on to fear, anger, and resentment will never make us happy or free. Harboring these negative emotions is not a pathway to peace. Rather it is like a fast-spreading cancer and breeds more of the same. Sadly, we are the ones who suffer.

Our **feelings do not define us.** They are simply temporary moments of emotion to be felt and held, not stuffed or avoided.

Besides our learned tendency to fixate on the negative aspects of life—what we want but don't have, what we wish others would be or do to conform to what *we* want—what else is preventing us from enlightenment and inner peace or wisdom? What obstacles stand in the way of our continuous pursuit of inner peace, personal freedom, and happiness?

Three words: *greed, fear, and complacency.*

Our shared pain stems primarily from greed, selfish ambition, and the fear of sacrificing our ideals. These, along with many other manifestations of fear or denial, are temporary coping mechanisms to feel empowered and in control.

None are long-term solutions to create the peace or personal freedom we say we want but don't yet have. In fact, our unquenchable thirst for more, to always win or be right, only further separates us from the peace and freedom we so desperately want.

Our obsession with more is destroying our lives.

What we need is more humility and honesty, not more money or stuff or power or control. And that means we must learn how to become more vulnerable and transparent.

"The secret of happiness is freedom; the secret of freedom is courage."

Carrie Jones

Vulnerability is a Strength, Not a Weakness

In fact, the secret to happiness is learning to get honest with ourselves and to *become more vulnerable*. That can be scary, especially for those who think they don't know how. And, contrary to what you may have been conditioned to believe, it can be incredibly powerful. But, as the above quote from Carrie Jones validates, *freedom and happiness require courage.*

We're not going to die if we get honest with ourselves about our secrets and fears.

Yet all too often we act like we will, reacting in a myriad of unhealthy ways to perceived threats; that if we allow other ideas, cultures, attitudes, or people to enter our personal private worlds, we will somehow risk losing our identities, or values, culture, or more.

That's simply not true. Life and success are not zero-sum games.

But, when we dare to lower our walls, opening the blinds to the windows of our souls, we allow light to replace the cold darkness of our hearts.

Also, it is not uncommon in our quest for success to lose sight of the bigger picture. Our beliefs often cloud our judgement, allowing them to dictate our worth or perceived lack thereof. We compare ourselves to others and pass value judgements to justify our position and opinions—good or bad, better than or less than, right or wrong—which only further confirms our learned biases.

This is made evident in public, social, cultural, and religious circles around the world. And, as the Dalai Lama discussed in *Toward a True Kinship of Faiths: How the World's Religions Come Together*, **we must embrace a spirit of love and compassion.**

Additionally, since we're being honest, most of us are lazy, scared, and complacent.

Fear of failing or succeeding holds us back. We believe our lying inner critics and fail to grow. Instead of facing the Unknown, we stay stuck in our same ways of thinking, being, and doing.

In our complacency, we stay huddled inside our supposedly safe and secure bubbles—the inner circle of those who think, act, dress, and look like us. In doing so, we are robbing ourselves of the chance to truly become the enlightened beings many of us claim we want to be.

What if we changed our approach?

What if we cast aside any judgment of the *other* or ideas unknown and instead began to cultivate a culture of curiosity, starting with us? What if we genuinely became interested in people outside our bubble? Would we be happier? Would the world be a little less chaotic?

Someone once said, "If you argue for your limitations, you get to keep them."

If we are intentional and committed to a quest for peace and harmony, why not start with ourselves? Let's ask more questions rather than arguing our positions.

When we commit ourselves to meaningful pursuits like inner peace, unity, and happiness—and approach life with the wonder of a curious child—we begin to uncover endless opportunities to grow in knowledge, deepen our experiences, and expand our circles of connection.

In a nutshell, we are blocked by our failure to be more *open minded and curious* and to let go of customs, attitudes, beliefs and our perpetual need to feel in control.

Frankly, these coping mechanisms are not the solution to our collective pain and suffering. They are rooted in self-centered fear and they are killing us.

Surrender is a Solution

Our resistance to change, sometimes kicking and screaming like a toddler in a melt-down, is neither right nor wrong. It's what we know. I know first-hand from my struggles with addiction and alcoholism how difficult it is to let go. The good news is we are not alone nor are we toddlers. Millions share the common bond of addiction to one thing or another.

No matter how hard I tried to stop drinking on my own, I could not. For me, "I got this!" and persistent self-will were not a solution. It wasn't until I hurt so bad I thought I'd die that I reached out to recovery for help.

As soon as I surrendered, I began to heal.

When we're stuck in old patterns and trying to shield our fragile egos, it's easy for our view of reality to get a little warped. Such patterns, skewed by judgement and the false sense of security they offer, ultimately do more harm than good.

The problem with willful negligence and closed-minded norms is that they keep us stuck, prisoners of our past. They block us from fully experiencing the sunlight of the spirit in ourselves and others.

This stubborn resistance to hold on to the familiar impedes our ability to be curious, humble, compassionate or kind. Our refusal to let go or need to be right is the key driver of all types of conflict—personal, relational, cultural, or relational. This stubbornness is the source of our struggle for peace and lasting freedom.

However, not all resistance is bad. For one, it keeps us sharp.

But choosing to hold onto beliefs because we are afraid is not a recipe for success in any endeavor or goal.

In short, *"I got this"* doesn't work!

So, what might we do? Where do we start?

First, to be free we must master the art of *surrender, acceptance, and action.* We must learn to *let go* before we can receive. We must embrace who we are and what we have before we can discover our potential to contribute.

Next, we must develop and nurture a *humble spirit of kindness, compassion, curiosity and love for ourselves and others.* We must live by the Golden Rule: "to do unto others as we would have them do unto us

Whether we call ourselves Christian, Buddhist, Muslim, or Jew, or practice any other form of spirituality, can we agree that to know and live peacefully, we must embrace and follow a moral code driven by kindness, compassion, and love?

These are pillars we can embrace. They are free and do not require anything more of us than an attitude of *humility, gratitude, and compassion.* In other words, **there are no excuses to not nurture them.**

Joy is found when we embrace the space between extremes. When we learn to accept our differences and adopt a mindset focused on building bridges, not walls.

Joy is found when we chill out and embrace a life full of love, not hate.

When we stay open-minded and curious instead of judging or condemning.

True connection and unity happens when we embrace the things that make each of us unique—our stories, our cultures, our quirks.

That's where unity begins. Period.

A few words of caution before we go further. This book might be the primer you need to discover that which you already know, but for your own reasons, have been holding back or not letting go. It may also be the swift kick in the ass or the gentle nudge you need to find the courage to take your first step forward, *from fear into faith* or freedom from the bondage of self.

Wherever you are and whatever extremes you are currently facing, I hope you are bold enough to take a chance on you. To take a long hard look in the mirror and ask yourself *what can I do better?* And then to summon the courage to pray or ask for help and then to *step forward into the life you want you to live and away from the one you don't want.*

Manifestation: What Can We Learn From a Thousand Piece Jigsaw Puzzle?

Our thoughts and actions are like putting together a thousand-piece jigsaw puzzle—corners and edges first. Then we slowly add pieces that look as if they belong together, connecting them one by one, and slowly an image begins to take shape. It may even vaguely begin to resemble the point of reference on the puzzle box.

As we continue to assemble the puzzle, the pattern becomes clearer. Soon the pieces seem to fall into place almost on their own. You step back and look at how far you've come. Maybe you even feel proud for a moment looking at all the connected pieces that form the image you are trying to recreate.

But something is missing. There's still a big hole in the middle of the puzzle. You look at the remaining pieces and quickly fit them where they belong, closing that hole, piece by piece. But there's a problem. You're one piece short.

You look on your lap, your chair, the floor, the sofa…but it's nowhere to be found. Then your dad casually strolls over to the kitchen table, reaches in his pocket and with an impish grin says, "I believe you are looking for this." And he places the final piece to complete the puzzle.

That is a true story my mom told me years ago when I was a teenager. She and my grandma used to love putting together jigsaw puzzles. Big ones, with a thousand pieces. Often of serene landscapes or idyllic castles nestled on a verdant knoll overlooking a pond with geese. You get the idea.

They would make hot cocoa and spread the pieces out on the smooth dining room table. For a whole afternoon they methodically put it together piece by piece, while Grandpa watched football or boxing in the living room.

Even after the first time, they knew they would be at least one piece short. They didn't let it stop them. They worked with the pieces they had and didn't worry about any missing pieces because they knew where they were—in Grandpa's pocket.

Over time and with continuous practice, the courage, confidence, and certainty you seek will be revealed. Your quest for clarity is found in the quiet. Not from incessant study of ancient wisdom, scripture, or philosophy. Nor is it found by voraciously reading scores of self-help books on success, self-love, or purpose.

While they can certainly serve as guides, books like these are not the solution. But action is.

Lasting transformation can only be accomplished through three things: *Awareness, Acknowledgement, and Action*. These are the three pillars of *Awakened Enlightenment*. These are the steppingstones of the path you're desperately seeking. These are what we need to find inner peace; to learn how to embrace the space between extremes.

They are the path, and ***the path is the solution***.

It is not until you are advancing on the path as both an observer and participant that you will ever truly know or find your truths. To manifest or accomplish whatever it is you seek, you must first be bold enough to walk the path, then learn how to embrace the messy middle between extremes. This process requires practice and diligence.

True clarity isn't found in the poles of one extreme or another. It is found in the emptiness of ego, in the infinite unknown, the space between past and future.

Clarity is found, as Ram Dass and many other ancient philosophers and leaders have taught—**here, now**. Where we are. In the present. Fully aware and in a state of being, not doing.

Therein lies our predicament—we keep looking for love and inner peace or wisdom in places outside of us. We search for meaning in questions unasked or unknown. Worse, if we're completely honest, most of us don't yet know what we really want.

Soul-Searching Questions to Consider as You Proceed:

How can we find peace without suffering? How can I find enlightenment? Is there life after death? How can we merge being and doing to accomplish what we want without attachment to ego or results? How can we find or get what we want if we relinquish control? Is life really all about perpetual struggle? How can I be happy, joyous, and free?

Regardless of culture, ideology, theology, or belief, we all have questions like these. Many may argue that there is one right way and one wrong way.

Is there, really? Is life really that simple—this or that and nothing in between?

Of course not. That's ludicrous.

Yet how often do we fret about our shortcomings and failures, feeling we must punish ourselves because we messed up? Or, to quote a phrase from recovery, "driven by a hundred forms of fear and self-delusion" we squander our precious present with worries of potential future hazards, such as not having enough money to retire, or dying before we get to fulfill our dreams.

The fact is none of this type of thinking is helpful. In fact, most of our worries will never happen. They are merely figments of our imagination based on our outdated belief system.

So that begs the million-dollar question of souls like us—*What is our truth?* How will we know when we see it? Feel it? Live it?

Are our current beliefs merely ideals for us, not necessarily for all? Or is there a different opportunity based on love, compassion and kindness of ourselves and others?

This book offers an alternative to the status quo. It's a daring challenge and a very real opportunity for us to not only uncover what we want, and why we want it, but more importantly, to identify and implement the subtle and not so subtle shifts we need to make if we are to progress and improve. To ask ourselves, ***How can I shift my attitude and mindset from fear to love?***

In short, this book attempts to guide you to two great questions we all have but may not yet bold enough to earnestly ask or pursue: ***"How can I be a better human?" and "Will my life matter?"***

We'll get there, I promise.

It's going to require painstaking effort and courage, especially as you learn how to be more brutally honest with yourself and others. But freedom is feasible, if you want it bad enough and are bold enough to learn how to embrace it.

As we begin the painstaking journey of personal growth and transformation, I encourage you to **be kind to yourself.**

Also, understand that reducing stress and cultivating calmness is not an overnight matter. We've often spent years, perhaps decades, listening to the noise in our heads, often vacillating between the extremes, feeding the soul-sucking inner critics. It will take patience, practice, and time to become comfortable in the absence of chaos, especially if your life is currently ruled by fear.

Peace and Compassion are Not Theories, They are a Choice.

If we want to be free or ever hope to change the world, we must first change ourselves. Creating a world culture of unity based on love, compassion and kindness *must start with* each and every one of *us*.

This practical yet infinitely dynamic principle of taking personal responsibility for our own growth and development begins with this *one simple life-changing principle and practice:*

Chill.

Learn to embrace the space between extremes, starting with the space between your ears and the two-foot drop from your head to your heart and gut.

When you do, you will experience freedom and you will know peace.

Chapter 2: Beyond the Sunday Smile

"Love your neighbor as yourself."
Jesus

Beneath a clear blue sky, aboard a massive cruise line, enroute to Turks and Caicos with my wife, I started reading, His Holiness, The Dalai Lama's book, *Toward a True Kinship of Faiths: How the World's Religions Can Come Together.*

After reading the introduction, I set the book down and watched the massive ship's wake slowly disappear across the vast North Atlantic. Like a swaddled child, the gentle rocking of the big boat felt safe. Peaceful.

My thoughts drifted to my hippie upbringing and my own twisted spiritual path: my introduction to a higher power in recovery and my experience as a Christian for twenty years before leaving the church in 2019.

As I gazed upon the endless horizon, it hit me: Everything—from the time I pressed my dad to explain to me who God was, to my prickly response to hearing the word God in early recovery, to feeling like I never really measured up or was worthy in church, to Friday night Shabbat with our communal family, and later to hot-yoga, massage, meditation, and praying in a community circle for a miracle to heal a close friend's brother battling a blood disease—all of it served a purpose. *Everything is connected. God is everywhere*, even the rocks and trees, oceans and streams.

Decades later, I now understand that every spiritual experience I've had was designed to help me connect or reconnect. To a higher power. To myself. To others. Every tradition, practice, principle, or ritual pointed to the same path—love. To learning to love a God I don't always understand. Loving myself. Loving others. And beneath love, there lay one word that codifies and galvanizes it all: *trust*.

Returning to the Dalai Lama's book, I admired his courage and humility. In particular how throughout his life and during the course of writing the book, he intentionally sought out relationships with spiritual leaders from all faiths, theistic or not. *Especially* those whose religious or spiritual beliefs or practices differed from his own. In these humble conversations he was looking for similarities, not hell-bent on pointing out differences.

In other words, he was hungry to listen and learn. In the book, without judgement and maintaining his own core beliefs, he shares deep insights from these conversations and friendships to clearly articulate a message of unity. More specifically, how we can take better care of ourselves and each other by creating cultures of kindness and compassion.

Which brings me to the Sunday Smile.

There's a story you may have heard of an unbathed man, likely homeless, in worn and dirty clothes who wandered into a church and found a seat in the back. Congregants stared at him with contempt or avoided eye contact altogether. Some scooted away to a different row. Not one person bothered to ask if he needed anything, nor offered him water or coffee, or dared to strike up a conversation with him.

Essentially, he was ostracized before anyone bothered to ask him what his story was.

Even though they belonged to a church that supposedly believed in helping those less fortunate than them, people pre-judged him.

The worship band stopped playing and the pastor took center stage.

Grabbing the microphone, he began his sermon. He started with high praise and accolades of a man who would soon become their new pastor. He mentioned all the good he had done in his former community—helping single moms, addicts, and homeless people. He enthusiastically talked about a few projects the incoming pastor and his former congregation did: building homes on mission trips for the unhoused and poor in Mexico. How he and a team of contractors helped to repair roofs and mend fences of the homes of some low-income seniors in their neighborhood, whether congregants or not.

The pastor continued raving how this new pastor and his family were all-in and thrilled to meet the congregation and lead the church to better serve their community.

Several in the crowd leaned forward, eager, hopeful, expectant, and hungry to hear more.

The pastor continued singing the praises of this man, then abruptly, he paused.

He took a long beat before continuing.

"Ladies and gentlemen, I'd like you to meet your new pastor," and motioned to the seats in the very last row of the room.

At that, the man dressed in dirty clothes, with matted hair and a scraggly beard, stood up and slowly made his way to the front of the auditorium. With his back slightly hunched, he gingerly ascended the steps of the stage.

Murmurs and whispers spun throughout the pews.

The man briefly glanced at the hushed crowd, then shook the pastor's hand, before standing behind the lectern, mic in hand.

You could've heard a pin drop.

Ashamed, some in the audience began to weep.

Soon the sniffles subsided and the new pastor spoke.

In a deep, clear, resonant voice, he addressed the crowd, "This church, under my leadership, will be one that opens its arms to anyone in need, including every one of you. We are here to make a difference and that starts with self-examination and attitudes. About how we think, act, and behave, especially toward those we don't know or like. I want each of you to go home and think about this moment and never, ever forget it. And, if today feels heavy on your heart, I would like you to pray for the courage and willingness to do better next time. I'll see you next Sunday."

Gently, he replaced the mic and walked off stage.

Many years ago, I read a quote by philosopher and theologian, Herbert Spencer. It has been a plumbline for me when I find myself drifting into gossip or judgment. It reads:

"There is a principle which is a bar against all information, which is proof against all arguments, and which cannot fail to keep a man in everlasting ignorance—that principle is contempt prior to investigation."

Chapter 3: Fail First, Fast, and Frequently

"Success is not a reward and failure is not a punishment."
Chögyam Trungpa Rinpoche

"Guilt, it's what's for dinner."

This was one of the smart-ass ad slogans I came up with in my youth after hearing about some of the shame and guilt laid on others who are less than perfect, especially in religious context.

Guess what?

We are not perfect.

And, whether you believe it or not, we are perfect as we are.

But that doesn't mean we stop trying to improve. It does, however, mean that we do not need to let fear and guilt and shame or blame control how we feel about ourselves.

The world isn't out to get us.

We do that well enough on our own with our without anyone else's help!

We are perpetual works in progress and I'm OK with that. But the question is, are you OK with it?

There is enough shame and guilt to pave the world a hundred times over. And whether you believe in original sin or not, every single one of us has our faults and secrets and shortcomings.

It comes with the territory of being human. And whether a root cause or not, it's all deeply connected to some form of fear.

The interesting thing though is most of what we fear is a lie, including fear itself.

Near the top of the list of common fears is our unnatural and unrealistic expectations about success, especially the fear of failure or rejection.

Failure is normal and necessary for growth. Yet for some reason it's gotten a bad rap. Instead of accepting that making mistakes are a natural part of life and learning, we falsely believe that they are "bad" or "wrong."

 Not true.

We've bought into a false narrative that equates our worth with not making mistakes and as a result, we suffer.

Worse, we exacerbate the problem.

Speaking from personal experience, to cover my butt and protect my pride for fear of getting "found out," I've often acted out in all sorts of absurd ways. For example, working harder, procrastinating, denying, or distracting myself with social media and other forms of escape, like in my past with drugs and alcohol.

Decades ago, I learned one of the most powerful and expensive lessons of life:

Escape is not a solution to failure or fear. Courage is. Responsibility is.

By themselves our behaviors may not immediately affect anyone else, But inevitably, they harm us and others.

The problem is that our avoidance or over-compensating behavior often directly and indirectly creates relational brick walls.

In other words, trying to be perfect and never fail isn't healthy.

All too frequently, in our attempt to hide our feelings of fear, doubt, or other insecurities, we create self-imposed prisons that keep us stuck and effectively prevent us from connecting with others.

Nobody wins when we're afraid of losing or failing.

Besides mastering the art of surrender, we must also learn how to reframe our perspectives about fear of failure and success.

In other words, we need to stop focusing on the extremes of winning or losing—the hero or zero syndrome; the all or nothing mentality that plagues so many of us and is further perpetuated by the vast majority of self-help books.

Instead, we must shift our focus to the path beneath our feet and then make a grown-up decision which way we want to go.

This requires courage and learning to trust ourselves and others.

The question then is how do we build trust?

It's not by controlling our emotions or hollow attempts to control others. Trust comes from understanding. From acknowledging our similarities. Knowing we all want the same thing—to be loved, accepted, and respected—to feel like we belong.

The superglue of building trust happens when we love and accept others as they are not as we want them to be. Trust is built by becoming vulnerable enough to risk our pride and ego and admit that we don't have all the answers.

Trust comes when we're humble enough to ask for help.

This is not easy and requires willingness and a shit-ton of courage. We must be willing to suck at first and accept that we will get better as long as we don't give up too soon.

The bottom line is that trust is a two-way street. We build it by first learning how to trust ourselves. That comes only from being willing to fail fast, first and often.

Are you beginning to see how this all works?

It's not about what others think of us or what others do or don't do. Our success ultimately depends on what we think of ourselves.

Now, let's examine and explore how we can leverage the tools and gifts we already have. Then let's use our imaginations to expand the dreams and visions of who we are now to visualize who we might want to become, knowing and accepting that this process will not happen overnight.

Failure is a Prerequisite of Success

To succeed, we must fail first, fast, and frequently. That's right folks, *if you want to grow, you need to let go.*

Specifically, you need to let go of:
1. Your need to be perfect.
2. Attaching your identity to what you do.
3. Allowing your fears to inhibit your desire for change and growth.

4. Thinking you are a failure just because you failed.

5. The idea that your value and worth are tied to whether you succeed or fail.

Each of the above shapes how we relate to ourselves, others, and the world. They are filters or lenses that can be changed, but because of the deep connections in our brains and patterns of behavior, have become defaults or blind spots that we seldom think about unless challenged.

Some of us need to be challenged. To ask ourselves, what I can do differently? What will it take to become the type of person I like to be around? How can I be more empathetic and understanding?

Let's face it, we all judge others who are different than us. I don't know why this is. Perhaps it's because we're hard-wired for survival; to be wary of anything or anyone foreign to us and as a potential threat. Regardless, I still look at others and form snap judgements about who they are and whether I'd like them based on mostly superficial input about their looks, clothes, posture, and demeanor.

Let's also be realistic, carefully considering the enormous space between our ideal images of success and where we are now.

Lastly, let's develop and implement strategies to change and rewire what we think and say to ourselves and others when things don't go our way or when faced with fear.

In other words, *let's grow up*.

For your consideration to practice:

What are some areas of your life where you feel inadequate?

In what three areas could you relax your need for control?

List three things that you have been putting off because you:

1. Don't want to do them.
2. Are concerned that they may require more time than you have.
3. Are worried that you must do perfectly or you will feel like a failure.

Now, ask yourself:

1. What's the worst thing that could happen if you don't do them?

2. What's the best that could happen if you did do them?
3. How do you think doing them would improve your life?

Take a breath and find the guts and decide to take one action to doing at least one of them **now.**

Pay attention to how it feels to make a decision and get into action, then take another step forward, and another. Habit stacking as James Clear calls it in *Atomic Habits*.

As you practice, you will become happier, less uptight and start the process of winning rather than staying stuck in a failure mindset. Also, if you choose to do nothing, stop worrying about it. Own it, and then move on.

Become Brave Enough to Suck at Something New

Success is a deeply personal and subjective measure. It's not exclusive, reserved for the elite few who conquer more personal demons or win more arguments or championships, trophies, or sales contests than the rest of us. *Life is not a race and success is not a destination.*

You know this.

Why then do you still struggle with confidence or believing that you don't have what it takes to succeed?

I can't answer that for you.

But for me, through decades of self-examination and practice, I've developed tons of tools to use and move forward. Now, I relish every opportunity I get to share them with those who are hungry to learn.

Success is whatever you choose it to be. And failure is one of many steppingstones on your path to success; toward enlightenment, understanding, awakening or whatever it is you claim you want to be, do or have, that upon getting it, will make you feel successful.

That's it.

Success is for those who seek to better understand the balance of life, who understand that it's human to make mistakes. It is found in the detritus of failure; the crumpled pages of shitty first drafts that litter the floor; the swings and misses in baseball; the skinned knees from repeated falls while learning to ride a bike, and the bumps and bruises on our face as we learn how to walk.

Think about it.

Have you always been good at whatever you do for a living?

What was it like to ask someone out on a date for the very first time? Or take your driving test? Or to take the MCATs or Bar exams? Did you pass the first time? If you didn't, did that mean you were a failure? No. More likely you learned what your mistakes were, made some adjustments, and tried again, and again, until you figured it out. Until you passed.

When our fear of failure is greater than our desire or reason to succeed, most of us will chose not to even try. And, when we do, we stay stuck.

The converse is also true—when our reason to win (our why) is greater than our fears, we will find a way to move from where we are to where we want to be. Some call this "gifts of desperation." I call it boldness, courage, conviction.

Call it whatever you like but understand this: *No progress can ever occur without failure or mistakes.*

Our fears of failure or success or any number of other learned and controllable anxieties are like a virus. Unless and until we take measures to promote better health, we will get sick. Our self-esteem will suffer and we will continue to point fingers or vacillate between the highs and lows of life believing that such extremes are acceptable.

In fact, according to several studies, more than 85% of us suffer from some form of low self-esteem.

Manifested as various forms of controllable fears, such as OCD, overthinking, procrastination, fear of intimacy, fear of rejection, fear of failure, and the dreaded imposter syndrome, we struggle with self-confidence and denial. Caught in a spin cycle of fear, we often run from one extreme to another.

Or we create unhealthy habits to overcompensate for our perceived shortcomings such as working too much, planning, procrastination, analysis paralysis, or denial and avoidance. Eventually we can't keep up and we get burned out from trying to show the world how together we really are. Soon, we collapse on the sofa curling up in a ball with a bowl of ice cream and hoping our anxieties and problems will all magically disappear.

That's not gonna happen.

Rubbing a brass lamp ain't gonna grant you your three wishes.

So, what's the problem and what might we do about it?

With the exception of medically diagnosed mental illnesses, **most of our fears are not real.** They are **F**alse **E**vidence **A**ppearing **R**eal.

We need to understand this and accept it. Then we need find the guts to get to work.

What if we set our pride and ego for a moment and stopped playing the victim? What if we attempted to let go of the five things I mentioned earlier? Rather than blaming our circumstances on others or our situation what if instead we chose to focus on and work toward a solution, accepting in advance that we will likely fail several times before we get it right?

How might that help us to become more confident? To fear failure less? To accept the simple fact that practice and failure are integral to success.

How might this bring us peace? Improve our relationships?

How do we do this? What steps do I need to take?

It depends.

How bad do you want a different outcome? How willing are you to try and fail until you succeed? Are you willing to do some work and let the universe take care of the results? Can you sit still and be patient enough for the answers you seek to come to you?

And the biggest question of all, are you willing risk your pride and ego and accept that you may not have the answers you want, yet?

This is what it means to embrace the space between extremes.

When the Student is Ready, the Teacher Will Appear

Learn to think of failure as a teacher, a wise master like a sensei, or Miyagi from Karate Kid , or the dude from

Kung-Fu, who said when you snatch the pebble from the hand, then you are ready.

Failure is a master instructor for those who have a growth mindset.

Some of the most successful people we know got their master's degrees from *the school of hard knocks*. They took every mistake, misstep, or failure in stride moving one step closer to success. In other words, they continue to learn from their failures and don't allow them to control them or sabotage their dreams and goals.

Many successful people came from broken homes or had some challenge in their youth that they were determined to overcome. They were fighters. They had a dream and knew why they wanted to change or where they wanted to go and then became humble and vulnerable enough to ask for help, follow advice, and get their reps in.

They never gave up. They didn't magically become experts overnight. Nor will you.

Before we can master anything in life, we must fail first and fail often. Those who fail faster usually are the ones who grow faster too.

And there is another side of the coin we cannot ignore. Sadly, some of us grew up with teachers, parents, or others who tore us down rather than built us up.

Telling us we're not good enough. That we were "working below potential." That we should or shouldn't do this or that. That *xyz* is a sin. And *we believed them.* To cope, many of us desperately seek ways to escape our pain.

Many lack the support of loving or supporting parents, teachers, and friends, or encouragement from a coach or boss. The scars of youth can be ugly and thick.

How sad.

And to add to our dilemma, those of us who experienced a shitty childhood have a hard time receiving feedback or constructive criticism. Instead of hearing the intent, we become defensive and take it personally. Regardless of what is said or how the message is delivered, we have built-in filters that only reinforce deep-seated **false belief systems** of our youth—*that we are not good enough. That we are not worthy. That we suck and are failures.*

We are not failures and we don't suck.

Goldilocks Syndrome

Perfection is a myth. For a control freak like me who came from a broken home and wants everything in my world to be "just right," I must learn to accept the fact that I:

- Will never be perfect
- Don't need to attempt to control everyone and everything in my world
- Can change my attitude about failure and become curious and adaptive rather than fearful and resistant to perceived pain of change or failure
- Decide to embrace all my mistakes and reframe them as teachable moments rather than a personal affront to my perceived worth or value.
- Embrace all that is, as it is, and approach every failure as an opportunity to learn and grow and every success as a lesson to be shared.

Mistakes, missteps, and mishaps are not bad. The sooner we stop resisting failure and start embracing it, the faster we will improve.

All major discoveries and breakthroughs in life happen after repeated failures. Even though we know this, why are so many of us still afraid of failing?

Because our thinker is off.

When we screw up, many of us tend to take it personally.

Guess what, it's not all about us. So, why do we waste so much time worrying about doing or not doing something?

The simple answer is *fear*.

Fear that we are somehow less than or inadequate if we don't get it—whatever *it* is—right the first time. That we are stupid or lame if we don't succeed immediately.

Life and success don't work like that.

I have spent my entire life searching for success. Vacillating between extremes of award-winning accomplishment and feeling like a total loser. *Hero to zero syndrome*, though that may be a misnomer, as I don't believe it has been recognized as a mental health condition per se. Regardless, every one of us struggles with all-or-nothing thinking.

There are many reasons why most of us never feel successful or have shitty relationships.

Most of these reasons are lies.

Again, this book aims to change that. To literally flip the script in your head and give you a framework that you can use wherever you are on your journey and whenever you want. It starts with your willingness and commitment to make some subtle shifts in your attitude and perspective.

Practice, Patience, Perspective, and Persistence

Practice is the panacea to inadequacy. *Patience* is what we find when we detach from one extreme or another and learn to wait in the in-between. *Perspective* is our attitude and approach to opportunities or problems.

Our attitude is energy.

And the energy we bring to an opportunity or challenge is the energy we get out of it. *Persistence* is what this chapter is all about. It's about all of it, patterns, processes, awareness, and learning to lighten up and take things in stride. It's really about learning how to shift our focus from perfection to progress.

Each of these require us to *become humble, teachable.* This is the magic skill we must learn and master if we are to fully grasp the enormous power found in the spaces between extremes. Mastery of these four traits (*Practice, Patience, Perspective, and Persistence*) is vital to our ability to lead and to create meaningful and lasting relationships others.

Again, to succeed, we must first be willing to fail.

Chapter 4: Deeper Awareness

"To know thyself is the beginning of wisdom."
Socrates

I believe who we are and who we become is a product of five things:

1. Our upbringing.
2. Our experiences.
3. Our environment.
4. Our inner spirit, curiosity, and creativity.
5. What we believe and how we respond to all of the above.

Each of the above shape how we relate to ourselves, others, and the world. These filters or lenses are changeable, yet our ingrained behavioral patterns often creates blind spots, which are rarely considered unless directly challenged.

Just as life isn't all black or white, neither is it all about fight or flight. Yet, if we are not careful, we can easily slip back into caveman mentality, ever vigilant, in a perpetual state of fear.

I know there is more to do if I sincerely want to be a better human. I have an obligation to pay closer attention to how I think and what I say or believe about myself because it directly and indirectly influences how I relate to God, myself, and others.

More specifically, on a personal level, I can improve in these areas:

- Mind
- Body
- Spirit
- Emotions
- Relationships
- Kindness
- Compassion
- Curiosity
- Leadership
- Love

It's no secret that *when we change the way we think* and *what we choose to believe*, our world changes. Our perspective shifts as we replace outdated beliefs about ourselves with new ones. And, according to neuroscience, everything we believe is tied to patterns we have created in our minds, to what we chose to believe.

The first step for us to evolve and move beyond our limiting habits and patterns is *awareness*; to identify the challenge or opportunity so we can grow and improve.

This premise makes two huge assumptions:

1. That what we are doing now isn't bringing us the joy and peace we say we want.
2. That the pain of staying the same is greater than our fear of change.

Each of the ten areas above represent opportunities for us to not only pay closer attention to our habits, attitudes, and beliefs, but also to examine and *decide which we want to work on now*.

There is no perfect way to do this other than for you to look at the list and assess which areas are causing you the most pain right now and determine what might happen if you were to invest your energy on finding a solution rather than staying unhappy and stuck.

I'm not going to unpack each of these, that's up to you. But I don't want to leave you hanging, so, please allow me to share some further insights and a deeply personal life-changing story to bring this all together.

Before I dive into the deep-end of the pool, something completely unexpected just rocked me to my core. I was all set to replay and relive a story I've told a hundred times when I was interrupted by Eminem and Skylar Grey's song, "Temporary," off Eminem's latest album, *The Death of Slim Shady*. I temporarily took my hands off the keyboard and allowed the weight of his words to illuminate a part of my heart I didn't know needed light.

His heart-felt lyrics and vulnerable interjections and exchanges with his daughter reminded me of the most painful conversation I ever had in my life: telling my son that his mom and I were getting separated.

That was over sixteen years ago and I hadn't thought about it in years. But that one song brought me back… to the ocean….the waves….that beach…and the look on my son's face, as if it was yesterday.

I had sworn I would not abandon my son as my dad had me, my mom, and younger brothers when I was twelve. My dad leaving without saying goodbye was the source of so much pain before I found recovery. Despite my will to not repeat the mistakes of my father, I felt like a failure. And I had to face my son and swallow my shame.

It hurt so bad.

Despite my best efforts to honor my commitment to my wife and son, my first marriage failed.

But unlike my dad, I didn't run away. I was there for nearly every one of my son's baseball games, concert performance, his graduations, and so much more.

Until recently, the pain still lingered deeply inside.

Two years ago, after a wonderful Thanksgiving meal with family, as my son was leaving, he stopped to give me a hug goodbye and said something I will never, ever, forget:

"Dad, thank you for all you and mom sacrificed for me. I love you."

The song, "Temporary," was exactly what I needed to hear in this moment. I closed my eyes and fully felt the emotions. I let the tears roll down my cheeks and didn't die.

If you get nothing more from this book, get this, **be aware of the opportunities to fully feel and experience the full breadth of human emotions.** Learn to welcome them as you would a dear friend or loved one who visits. When there is a knock on the door to your heart, open it. Let them in. Welcome every emotion with open arms as you would your child who says, "I love you."

The magic lives in the unexpected miracles and music of your soul singing.

Hear it. Feel it. Embrace it.

Came to Believe

I came to believe a long time ago that **there are no mistakes in this world.** That **everything happens for a reason.** I believe it is my responsibility to pay close attention to and learn from my personal struggles. To try my best to adapt and make adjustments to improve my attitude, thoughts, or actions so that I may have a different outcome.

What started as a drive to become a better writer and more confident speaker and salesperson evolved into this quest for boldness. To become willing and honest enough to acknowledge my strengths and weaknesses in terms of skill, ability, and habits. And to embrace the ones I like and find the courage to change those I don't.

I began practicing daily reflection and introspection. Slowing down, learning to chill. Some days that included reading something spiritual, others included periods of prayer and meditation. Still others, mostly on weekends, I would clear my head on long hikes along the Point Reyes National Seashore, hoping to find the right thought or inspiration for the then current book I was writing—*Ten Seconds of Boldness.* I would pray, meditate, and ask the universe or God for direction as I put one foot in front of the other along scenic coastal paths to places like Alamere Falls or Sculptured Beach.

Several employee satisfaction studies show a greater emphasis being placed on internal measures of success, especially with regard to a sense of belonging and recognition.

Akin to climbing Maslow's Hierarchy, there's a clear trend toward personal growth, spiritual enlightenment and awakening. In addition, issues-based goals to increase cultural awareness and affect change—particularly relationships and social justice—are fast becoming new barometers of success, especially for the next generation of leaders.

The yin and yang of what success means is best interpreted by those who seek it. I know that my self-esteem and self-confidence are strongest when I am doing the things I believe will help me solve a problem or accomplish a goal.

I find the greatest joy when I am helping others. Sharing my experience, strength, or hope through my recovery story. Or, as a coach or consultant, guiding individuals and businesses to discover their passion and purpose while teaching them ways to become better humans.

So much of what we struggle with in life seems to come back to belief and willingness or lack thereof. Of humility, focus, and awareness—to pay attention and ask for help when necessary.

Most of us don't want to look in the mirror or take a look at where we may be coming up short. At work. In relationships. Of our perceptions of success. But until we have the courage to take an honest look at ourselves and become willing to do some things differently, we will remain where we are, stuck.

I know what this feels like. I was only ninety days sober and the compulsion to drink had not yet been removed. Frustrated about what I thought was lack of progress, I feared the worst and worried I might drink again. And for me, if I drank again, I could die.

Thank God I had a sponsor who saw me slowly spiraling back into my disease and who cared enough to help me do something about it. It wasn't until a beautiful spring day in May that everything changed.

"We need to do your third step," he said. "What are you doing this Saturday?"

The Miracle of Letting Go

One of the most important and life changing steps in my recovery was the third step. It's premise is all about turning my will over to a power greater than myself and trusting in that unseen power as a spiritual means to overcoming my addiction.

I'll never forget the day I did mine with my sponsor, Bobby B.

"Shawn," Bobby started, "you have been carrying around a lot of crap. It's like a sack full rocks—all your guilt, shame, doubt, worry, anxiety, and fear. And it's weighing you down. Everything that stands in the way of you being able to get over the mental obsession and compulsion to drink."

I stared at the dirt. I knew he was right.

"Here's what we're going to do," he continued. "See that garbage can over there near the church? We're going to kneel in front of it and hold hands and say the third step prayer. That is the third step. But before we do, I want you to close your eyes and feel how heavy all those rocks are. Then I want you to imagine walking over to that garbage can, lifting the lid, and dumping that entre sack of rocks in the trash."

I did as he instructed.

"You got it?" he asked. Again, I nodded, "Great. Now I want you to slam the lid shut and let that shit go."

I laughed and followed his instructions explicitly. We then said the third step prayer out loud. As we were reciting it—two guys holding hands in broad daylight, kneeling on a dusty hillside beside a church near a garbage can—I experienced a miracle. In that moment, all the fear and worry and anxiety and compulsion to drink was lifted!

A wave of chills rippled across my arms, and I wept.

In that moment I experienced freedom for the first time in my young adult life.

It was a miracle; one I'll not soon forget.

I often go back to that dusty hillside and that garbage can when the weight of other burdens seems insurmountable. Now, I do the same thing as I did then—I lift the lid, dump the rocks, and after reciting the third step prayer in my head, I slam the lid shut and let that shit go!

Nothing Changes Until Something Changes

Miraculously, saying the third step prayer with my sponsor that day took away my compulsion to drink. But I had a very specific problem and my sponsor knew a very specific solution to help me escape my negative spiral.

But that isn't the only challenge I've faced.

One of my biggest has been my tendency to overthink things. To fret about past mistakes (guilt or shame) or worry (fear) about what hasn't happened yet.

None are productive and all are extremes that keep me from fully enjoying the present.

Just as there are endless opportunities for us increase our awareness about things we may want to be or do better, there are a multitude of tools, tips, and techniques to help us become more aware. Some, including the twelve-steps of recovery and my own five-step method (*identify* the problem/opportunity, clearly *decide* what you want, know *why* you want it, write a clear *plan*, and *start working that plan*), have proven to help me feel more secure with who I am while also giving me the skills to avoid cultural and inherent gravitational pulls toward one extreme or another.

If you read the news or engage with social media, you know the pull to divide us is real. But we get to choose what we read or believe. I do my best to choose wisely.

Other self-care methods I have found helpful include yoga, hiking, meditation, writing (especially journaling), therapy, counselling, and other spiritual practices.

All help me to increase my awareness or inspire me to change something—diet, attitude, behavior, etc. All have also proven beneficial when I approached them with a solution-based mindset.

But here's the cold truth: **All the tools in the world are useless unless you use them.**

None of the techniques you may learn can help you until you practice them. I like how Dalai Lama XIV puts it, *"Change only takes place through action, not meditation and prayer."*

There is great wisdom in the above quote.

Unfortunately, we tend to think too much. We have a natural proclivity to excessively ruminate (replay) our past mistakes and shortcomings, or future trip (worry) about what *might* happen.

What a complete waste of time and energy!

It's no wonder so many of us feel stressed out and exhausted.

Chapter 5: Admit, Accept, and Adapt

"This above all: to thine own self be true,
And it must follow, as the night the day,
Thou canst not then be false to any man."
William Shakespeare, Hamlet

I was losing my mind and needed therapy.

Several years ago, I was struggling with some inner demons that I felt should have been gone a long time ago. I was replaying past hurts, pain and anger, mostly around fear of abandonment issues from my childhood. My resentments toward my father and myself were blocking me from intimacy with my new wife.

At the urging of my sponsor, I started weekly counselling.

Five years and a whole lot of tears later, I finally broke through the anger to the sadness and fear and ultimately landed in a place of love and forgiveness.

Afterward, I understood and then sought to forgive my father and myself.

There are many angry people in this world. The current and growing animosity and divisiveness over politics and religion have further driven a wedge between people who in actuality are much more alike than different.

We all long to be happy, loved, accepted, and to live good lives. Yet, beneath our outbursts (public or private), or fake smiles, are many layers of fear.

Inside we struggle to not lose our shit and keep up a good front to not rock too many boats. **Sometimes the boat needs to be rocked if we ever hope to get to the other side.**

When we focus on the negative, we remain stuck, knee-deep in our own shit.

But when we change our focus and perspective, looking at each challenge as an opportunity for growth to become more enlightened, awake, and emotionally mature, our whole world can change.

We must learn to *understand, admit, and accept* that on the other side of the storm are clear skies. Beyond the darkest hours, dawn.

Just because today is raining doesn't mean the sun no longer exists.

From those five years of therapy and thousands of hours in recovery meetings, I learned that the solution would not come instantly. Life doesn't work like that, especially for the important stuff like love and relationships.

It took many years to heal the hurt and pain I felt around my dad leaving me. I was faced with more opportunities to apply what I'd learned decades earlier while blending families after divorcing my first wife and marrying my new best friend. I feared I may push my new wife away with my deeply entrenched belief systems and own insecurities about intimacy.

The difference though was I was aware of it and was willing to grow and change to communicate and connect on a deeper level with Crissi, her kids, and my son.

It wasn't easy but after another ten to twelve years of marriage and lots of communication practice, I can honestly say that our relationship has never been stronger.

Why is this important?

Because our ability to lead or realize our full potential is limited by our resistance or refusal to change. Our failure to recognize or admit our own shortcomings, and our unwillingness or vehement refusal to become more curious about others whose views differ from our own, prevent us from truly connecting with others.

But we can change, if we want to.

World unity and peace depend on our commitment to greater kindness, compassion, and love for each other.

It starts with honesty—becoming more honest with ourselves and others. Nothing will ensure our serenity and ability to connect and build healthier relationships more than rigorous self-examination and honesty.

Acceptance

Thriving, personally and professionally, requires honesty, humility, and self-reflection. We must be authentic and vulnerable.

On the surface, rigorous reflection, self-awareness, and brutal honesty appear simple and easy. They truly are, once we let go of our ego and self-deception.

Though humbling, acceptance is a key to us overcoming feelings of imposter syndrome. Getting honest with ourselves is like a power boost for personal growth and transformation. Best of all, it's a habit that can be learned.

Let's explore this deeper by giving you some practical tools for greater self-awareness.

Honesty Equals Peace of Mind

Getting honest with yourself is the best thing you could possibly do for your happiness, confidence, and peace of mind. Without a willingness to take an honest, non-judgmental look at who we are and who we want to be, and then identify the obstacles in our path, we will never get better. We will forever remain stuck in the prison of our own minds and may become bitter or angry at ourselves, and those closest to us. Worse, our stubborn resistance to change may cause us to spiral into the dark pit of hopelessness and despair, resigning ourselves to the belief that all this effort is a waste of time.

I've been there. And it flat out sucks.

I hope and pray you become brave enough to face your own personal critics and teach them a new language. One of hope and possibility. Of confidence and success.

Self-awareness is all about honesty. It's about developing character, mindset, virtuous traits, and habits that build up rather than tear down our self-esteem. Healthier self-esteem comes from practice, repetition, and discipline until we form a new habit.

This process never ends.

And it is easier when we approach such change with curiosity and an open mind.

As you continue to practice, you will discover more about what you value and where you need to improve. You'll be more apt to refine your character, your belief systems, and your conduct so you may reduce and minimize your negative traits and expand those which serve the greater vision of who you or your higher power wants you to be.

Curiosity, Conviction, and Courage

I doubt I'm the only one that has difficulty staying focused or motivated, especially when there are lots of things to do that either don't seem like fun or are new and uncomfortable.

We all resist change.

To help retrain your brain and help wean you from your natural proclivity to vacillate between extremes or resist change, let's get dig a little deeper.

I call this *the honesty exercise.*

Consider each of these questions:

1. What do you think you want and why?
2. What are you good at or like to do?
3. What do you not like about yourself and why?
4. What are you grateful for?

5. What is holding you back?
6. What excuses do you keep making for where you are in your life?
7. Why do you think you continue to make them?
8. What continues to cause you stress?
9. What would you like to change or eliminate?
10. What have you done to change?
11. If fear was no longer a problem, what are you willing to do to get what you want?
12. What does "success" look and feel like to you?

This is not a complete list of introspective questions. Only you know what you want or need. Feel free to add or customize them to your unique situation, wants, needs, or opportunities.

To get the most out of this exercise, it is imperative that you *complete the four-step process below for at least one question*, and after you do, notice any changes to your thoughts, attitudes, or emotions.

Action Steps:

1. Write down your immediate response to each of the questions. *Don't overthink them.*

2. Pay close attention to how each question and your answer makes you feel. For example, question #3 above: What do you not like about yourself and why? What feelings does this question evoke? Where, in your body, do you feel it? Describe the feeling. For example, when I think about my tendency to bowl over Crissi, I feel a tightness in my gut and a lump in my throat. I feel sad because I love Crissi and don't like it when I say or do things that upset her.

3. Ask yourself, *What is this trying to teach me (embrace and accept it) and what can I do to change? (action).*

We'll cover action in the next chapter, but for now **write down and commit to one thing you can do now** and then go on to the next question.

Assess any shifts or changes to how you feel or what you've decided after completing this process for each question. Make a decision to what you will do differently, if anything.

Extra Credit #1: For questions #5, #6, #8, and #9 draw a circle and write down all the answers that immediately pop into your head. Look at them and ask yourself *what can I do now to change my attitude or let them go?*

Extra Credit #2: Do the same thing for Questions #2, #4, and #12, only list your assets and opportunities and potential benefits of change.

The purpose of this honesty exercise is to *become more aware of your patterns of resistance to change.* **Don't let your fears or excuses hold you back.**

This isn't a race or contest. You can come back to these questions and the mental and somatic awareness exercise whenever you want or feel you need to. Remember to give yourself some grace as you practice and grow.

Side note: I learned steps three and four from some intense work with my award-winning, Somatic Life Coach, Devon Carter. She also taught me some simple movement exercises similar to Tai Chi that have helped me get out of my head and remain centered and grounded whenever I practice them.

The key action phrase is *progress, not perfection.*

I encourage you to find or develop a routine or practice that works for you. One that can help you find the stillness between the extremes of your mind, body, and spirit. One that helps you chill.

Beware of Your Red Zones

What are Red Zones?

Red Zones can be patterns and habits you default to when facing uncomfortable situations. Procrastination is one all of us do. We put off doing things we know need to be done for a myriad of reasons, most of them based in some type of fear or anxiety. Rather than mustering the courage to press on we make excuses or avoid what we know needs to be done by surfing social media or the internet, binge-watching TV, compulsive cleaning, etc.

Rather than immediately running away from your fear, run into it.

Make a list of what needs to be done, one to three things and then do them, starting with the one you've been avoiding the longest.

Watch how liberating it feels when you *do one positive thing* to move you closer to what you want or complete something, like taxes, or cold-calls, or mowing the lawn, doing laundry, cleaning the garage, etc. that you've been putting off.

Every time I do what I know needs to be done whether I feel like it or not, I feel energized, empowered, and often end up knocking off two to three more things on my written or unwritten to do list.

There are many other Red Zones. Here are a few more and some simple acrostics I learned in early recovery which I still use today which you may find helpful prevent your worries, anxieties or fears, from controlling you or your emotions.

Pay Attention

As I mentioned earlier paying attention is half the battle, Again, when you catch yourself procrastinating, stop and ask yourself: *What are these feelings trying to tell me? What's really going on? Am I afraid of making the wrong decision or doing the wrong thing?*

Accept that you are not alone and it's normal to resist change.

Sadly, it has also become normal for many of us to vacillate between the extremes of all or nothing, success or failure, etc. To first avoid or seek entertainment of some form of escape to anything we deem "stressful" rather than doing what ought to be done.

Repeating the same negative patterns of avoidance or denial is insane.

To stop that habit, we need to do a few things differently. And we need to do different things.

Rather than take a chance on being wrong we are conditioned that we must have all the answers and that the risks of making a bad move could jeopardize our power, position, or credibility. Newsflash: we all make mistakes. Some of us are humbler and more willing to admit it when we ae wrong or don't know.

Decide now to stop running and start growing.

I can hear some of you saying, *Yeah, but you don't know what's at stake.*

You're right, I may not know the intimate details of your situation. But I bet your fears aren't as unique as you think they are.

Here are three acrostics that I'd like you to memorize and practice whenever you feel like you are in a Red Zone. They are self-explanatory.

- HOW
- HALT
- FEAR

HOW: This one saved my ass many times in early recovery and still helps me today.

Honesty

Open-mindedness

Willingness

Another is HALT. Don't get too:

Hungry

Angry

Lonely

Tired

And the last one, as I mentioned in chapter 3, is FEAR.

False

Evidence

Appearing

Real

Another acronym for fear is *fuck everything and run*. But that's what most of us already do and it's not helpful.

Let's return to the honesty exercise above and this notion of self-awareness and evaluation.

It's not fear that holds us back—it's the fear of feeling fear. When we learn how to *admit, acknowledge and accept* the fact that fear is normal and that most fears are not real, we can refocus our energy away from the extremes of yesterday and tomorrow and onto today. Here. Now. In this moment.

This is where true freedom is found.

Everything else is just noise.

Silence the noise.

Stop the insanity of thinking you have to do or be everything to achieve it all. Instead, live the life you were created to live and learn to be comfortable outside of the drama.

I get it. Our addiction to drama keeps pulling us back to gossip, abuse, drugs—anything that provides a temporary high.

We will never be happy in any extreme until we learn to love ourselves, and to be grateful for what we have and who we already are.

Everything I am sharing is based on decades of earned wisdom from making a shit-ton of mistakes.

The sooner we learn to strive for progress not perfection, the happier we will be. Conversely the sooner we unlock the handcuffs of our past—the shame and guilt and regret—and stop playing the victim, then and only then will we be truly free.

You are smart. You know all this already.

But each of us is on a different part of the same path toward enlightenment and awakening.

The suffering will continue as long as there is more to learn. Understanding this and accepting it makes it easier to fully grasp the concept of progress not perfection.

Now that you have invested some energy being honest and acknowledging the simple fact that you don't know it all nor will you ever, let's take another bold step forward.

Why is this so important?

Because if we want to be authentic leaders, teachers, coaches, and humans, we must find the courage to become more vulnerable.

We must share our imperfections.

But before we can do that, we need to *identify them, admit them, and accept them.* From there, we can begin the long and uncomfortable transformation from fear to confidence.

From avoidance to trust.

Becoming more transparent is the greatest skill anyone can learn to improve their personal and professional relationships.

The days of iron-fisted micromanagement no longer have a place in corporate America. Trying to control outcomes doesn't build trust. Perpetuating these archaic modes of leadership and communication is counterproductive; methods like these instill fear and don't foster collaboration or creativity. Because everyone is so worried about fucking up, productivity suffers.

What we need is to take responsibility for what we can control and stop pointing fingers and blaming others or institutions for our situation.

Ultimately, we need to accept that besides death, nothing is certain.

We cannot control outcomes or people or situations.

To thrive individually and as organizations, we must do the hard work of taking fearless and personal inventories of our own assets and liabilities.

For my twelve-step friends, we must complete a fourth step.

The key to all of this is not to go on a crusade as some politicians are wont to do, looking for dirt to smear opponents. This is deeper and more powerful than that.

We must examine who we are, what we believe and what we really like and don't like about ourselves. We must look at our fears, doubts, insecurities and resentments openly and honestly, and list them on paper.

We must also look at our relationships, especially strained or broken ones.

Whom have we hurt? Where are we at fault? What can we do differently?

This process is scary and requires great courage, trust, and faith to complete.

We must face the four-headed horsemen of pride, shame, guilt, and fear and stop feeding the beasts before they suck the life out of us.

It is only through admission, acceptance, and adaptation that we can move through these ailments which are holding us back.

Each of these are specific actionable processes to move us from fear to faith and hope. From pain to joy… etc.

As we embrace these steps, our life changes.

Final Thoughts For Now

In closing this crucial chapter, here are some final thoughts to prepare us for practical exercises to chill, reduce stress, and live more fully.

Admit:

Unless it will hurt someone else more, admit when you are wrong. For me, admitting when I'm wrong reduces stress because I don't have the burden of guilt or shame weighing me down.

Accept:

"It is what it is." One of my former co-workers often said this whenever she was faced with situations that were challenging or didn't go as planned. She didn't dwell in self-pity. Instead, she learned from the situation and took responsibility for what she could do better next time, then moved on. The key to acceptance is to develop the habit of having grace with yourself and understanding that mistakes are a normal part of life.

Adapt:

This is where our mettle is tested. If it's important enough, we will find a way to accomplish what we want. We will adapt out of necessity and because we have a big enough reason to want to. **If we don't have a big enough want, need, or desire, we won't change. Period.**

One of the greatest obstacles to our own success is our tendency to take simple solutions and complicate them. We think too much and act too little.

It's not rocket science!

If you are anything like me, you may overthink and overcomplicate things. Many believe that research and knowledge will change your life. News flash—it won't.

Meaningful change requires action.

Planning, research, and study are definitely important parts of that. But planning alone will not guarantee your success. Why? Because the best plans are flexible and adaptable.

We'll explore these ideas further in subsequent chapters. For now, can we agree that change is inevitable and that you have the power to control some of it?

Remember this: We will never rise above our fear and doubt until we muster enough courage to change and take the first step in a new direction.

I have learned that **my peace of mind is inversely related to my level of expectations about a desired outcome.** And my attitude is directly related to my level of acceptance. Instead of getting angry about something I can't control, I look within and try to see what it is that I can do differently. Again, I ask myself or pray, "What is this trying to teach me? And how can I master my response to it?"

Some days this comes easy for me. Others make me want to break glass in the recycling bin. And that's just the way it is.

Repeating this process of reflection and change has not only made me more self-aware (able to catch myself before I say or do something I'll later regret), but over time it has enabled me to shift my mindset away from problems and inconveniences to solutions and growth.

As a result, I am happier, healthier, and more confident. In many ways, I've matured and become more responsible, especially when it comes to admitting my own shortcomings and finding the courage and discipline necessary to change my old ways of thinking. Plus, I sleep better at night.

Chapter 6: Action

*"The magic you are seeking is in the action
you're not taking."*
Anonymous

Thus far, we've looked at some of the hurdles that stand between us and what we want. We've also explored a few ways we might turn our challenges into opportunities and stop or slow down the rollercoaster of emotion and fear between extremes.

In the previous chapter, I intentionally gave you some action steps for the sole purpose of helping you focus on solutions rather than problems. This process is called reframing, and it is tantamount to making the mental, physical, emotional, spiritual, and relational shifts necessary to become less stressed and more at ease with who we are or who we want to be. Reframing is also important to help us continue to evolve, and to not loiter in the infinite extremes of life.

Again, this doesn't make the extremes wrong, nor does it mean we are "less than" for making human mistakes. Reframing is a healthy and responsible practice that can illicit powerful transformation.

So far, we have focused primarily on the first step of my five-step process—*identify the problem or opportunity*. Now let's move onto step two, *clearly decide what you want*.

The Five-Step Method:

1. Identify the problem or opportunity
2. Clearly decide what you want
3. Know why you want it
4. Create a plan
5. Take action on that plan

Don't Let the Rats Steal Your Dreams!

When looking at problems and opportunities it's imperative that we approach them honestly while assessing what we want and what we don't want.

Equally important is step two: **Clearly decide what you want.**

Without clarity you will not be able to focus your energy on a specific goal or target.

Equally important is knowing what to let go of. Until we identify what we want an clearly decide what we're going to do to get it, we will continue to spin in circles, never really making any forward progress in our goals or relationships.

When we stay stuck in downward spiral, we suffer. Our relationships become transactional and stale. The zeal and zest for living disappears. Soon we put a dust cloth over our trunkful of dreams and stash it in the attic hoping the rats don't destroy whatever is inside.

Don't let the rats steal your dreams!

What, then, do we need next?

Before we leap right into action let's take a brief look at *decision-making, motives, and creating a plan.*

While each of the five step in my *five-step method* are dynamic, they are not always done in sequential order. However, it is crucial that you don't take any shortcuts. *For the process to work, you must do all five steps.*

Just as you cannot make leavened bread without yeast, so too, you must willingly and intentionally commit to practicing each step of the *five-step method* if you want to maximize the benefits you seek. The best way I know of to learn anything new is to not overthink or overanalyze it. Instead, find the guts to dive in and just do it.

Sound scary?

Good! That's means you have a chance to grow.

How can we make it *not so scary?*

Let's start with some decision-making practice. The first step to any action is always a choice or a decision. Sure, we need to take action for change to happen. But for some people, jumping into action isn't as easy as it seems. Many are afraid of failing or making the wrong decisions and therefore make none. While doing nothing is a choice, it won't create any meaningful change in your life.

For example: Let's say we want to lose weight or stop a habit or behavior such as drinking or gambling, what's the first thing we need to do? Make a decision to stop or change. Or make a decision to not change and live with the consequences.

Either way, you get to choose.

Decision Making Practice

1. Decide to *identify and admit* there's a problem
2. Decide *what you want* and what you're *going to do* about it.
3. Decide to *find out why* you want it.
4. Decide *what* you're *willing to do* to get it.
5. Decide to get into action and to never give up.

Hopefully you can see the progress you've already made with the first few chapters of this book. Life is quite simply a series of choices and decisions we make. Some are "good," meaning they benefit us or others, or they have a positive outcome. Others are "bad," meaning they didn't work out as we hoped for and perhaps hurt some people along the way.

Here's another hard truth: Some of us suck at making decisions.

As I mentioned earlier, too many of us are consumed by an unspoken need for certainty and perfection. As a result, we waste countless hours overthinking and worrying we will make a wrong decision. To save face and protect our pride, we often chose to do nothing rather than face our fears or risk our ego.

That's a choice we can all make and it's the easy way out.

If you want to grow, you need to go.

By go, I mean take a chance that you will fail and step forward into your fear rather than cower like a scared cat under the bed. I encourage you to push your boundaries and make more and tougher decisions.

If you want to lead you must learn how to not only confidently make decisions but also be willing to admit, at least to yourself, that you can always do better.

All of life is continuous improvement. There is no arrival.

Five Confidence Building Tips

Here are five suggestions to remember next time you have to make some tough choices:

1. Make a decision even if you don't have all the answers.
2. Don't overthink or second guess it.
3. Avoid analysis paralysis.
4. Commit and be willing to take risks.
5. Follow through with <u>action</u>, *not words*

Now, let's turn our attention to the third step, *why*. To motives. To inspiration. To drive and ambition. To all the things that are going to get us off our butts and into the game of life either because we must or because we have a desire or motive so powerful that we will not be denied.

Your Why is the Cornerstone to Your Success

This is one of the most critical sections in the whole book, because without a clearly defined why, we tend to give up too soon. We quit at the first setback or consider ourselves a failure because we didn't get what we thought we wanted in the time we expected to get it. In short, there are three primary blocks to our success:

1. Unclear motives
2. Unrealistic expectations
3. Impatience

Each of these also negatively influence our belief system—about what we believe we can or cannot do and what we perceive and believe about our skill level, resources, and abilities. Part of the problem, as I have mentioned several times, is *we think too much*. Overthinking is one more extreme that blocks us.

Our minds are cluttered with thousands of thoughts, most of them negative, which only exacerbate conscious or unconscious feelings of confusion, especially when it comes to establishing goals, creating plans, and finding our motives.

We are distracted by hundreds of trivial things which impede our forward progress. In some instances, the distractions are so large and prevalent that we have no clue how address them. To add to our dilemma, we don't know where to start. *We don't know what we don't know and, as a result, feel so overwhelmed that we do nothing.*

How do we find the balance between being, for example, a perfectionistic workaholic and a chronic procrastinator? One solution is to organize our lives and minds. Starting with getting rid of crap we don't need—physically and mentally—especially outdated thoughts beliefs, and attitudes.

An Organized Mind

Most of us have too much junk in our heads—fears, worries, doubts, appointments, obligations, deadlines, etc. Like an overstuffed garage, our minds become filled with hundreds of things we no longer use or need, such as broken TVs, outdated computers, old clothes that no longer fit, and scores of other things that have outlived their usefulness. As a result, we feel weighed down. Unmotivated, if not downright lazy. Worse, we keep wasting time thinking and worrying about shit we can't control, which only adds more stress.

Have I struck a chord? I hope so. Because like everything else thus far, there's more work to do. Let's start by making some decisions about what we need to keep and get rid of.

Out With the Old to Make Room for the New

It's time for a mental garage sale, a few trips to Goodwill, or a dump run. Time to get rid of old habits which are not fulfilling us so we can make room for creative energy necessary to pursue what we really want and to clarify why we want it. If you want to create space for calmness and clarity, you'll need to clear away the crap first.

When our motives are clear and our desire or need is great enough, most of us will get into action to do what needs to be done.

However, most people procrastinate and are not clear about what they want or what the perceived benefits are. We also tend to expect too much.

What's more, most of us have a confidence and belief problem: We are not sure if the effort will produce the results we want or are unsure of our ability and desire to put in the effort. Instead, we keep adding to the piles of crap already in our mental garage. Soon we can't find anything when we actually do need it. We are not motivated to clean it, so the garages (mental and physical) remain cluttered. *We remain scattered and unsure,* which further *impedes our ability to feel confident or productive.*

Hopefully we will wake up one day and say, "today's the day." Then make a decision to clear out our physical and/or mental garage.

Find a Reason That Matters to You a Lot

After my mom had neck surgery she required more care and needed to move in with us. Before she moved in, we needed a clear path so she wouldn't trip and fall.

In one weekend, Crissi and I cleared that sucker out and organized it enough to be safe, and to quell any potential comments from Mom about what a disaster it was.

Of course, we did this because we love my mom. But the reasons weren't completely altruistic. We had no choice. **We did it because we had to.**

Sometimes Our Why Finds Us Before We Find it

At the time all this happened, we questioned why. It wasn't a self-driven goal. It was inconvenient, and yet caring for my mom gave Crissi and me a *renewed sense of purpose*.

It provided an opportunity for Crissi to reevaluate her work situation where she was getting burned out. It allowed me to connect with my mom on a deeper level than I had in many years. It also made me grateful to work for company that supports family first values which gave me the freedom and flexibility to care for my parents.

Lastly, it gave Crissi and me a chance to work together caring for someone else. In the end, that made our relationship stronger. I mention this because we may not find our exact *why* by thinking about it. But, when we approach life with an open mind and a willingness to learn and love, we discover our why—or our purpose will find us.

Like anything worthwhile or valuable, nothing will ever change until we make a decision to change and commit to taking the first step toward what we want. Clearly deciding what you want is one of the most important action steps you can take.

Experience Makes Everything Easier

Update: All that work, prep, and care Crissi and I did for my mom a few years back has made it so much easier to prepare for her moving in with us this past winter.

For the past several years after she moved out the first time, the garage became packed with more crap. Over the last year, Crissi and I have been chipping away at the piles, not because we want to go through years of memories in dusty boxes. No, we are doing it because we want and need to make this space as comfortable and welcoming as possible for Mom. Knowing our why makes the work so much easier. So does the fact that we've already done this once.

The next time you feel tempted to procrastinate or avoid an unpleasant task, such as cleaning out the garage or doing a dump run, remember this story.

Resistance only makes tasks harder and creates unnecessary friction. You know what you get when there's too much friction?

Blisters.

Finding the Courage to Act

After decades of practice, I have discovered that in any uncomfortable situation it is my responsibility to find the courage to act. Those are two things I can control. However, I cannot control the outcome and I need to stop believing I can.

Years ago, I learned that *my inner peace and serenity are*, as I said before, *inversely proportional to my level of acceptance and expectation*. When my expectations for a particular outcome are not met, I become frustrated, irritable, and tend to "try harder."

Despite years of therapy and recovery, it's still not easy to be humble enough to admit my shortcomings or recognize where I need to improve.

Like you, I'm a work in progress.

When it comes to personal growth, I ask lots of questions, but don't always get the answers I want. I do, however, always get the answers I need. For example: How did I respond when things didn't go my way today? How do I feel and act when I don't get what I want? Do I sulk? Blame others? Give up? Am I so driven that I impose my will into a situation trying to make it work out the way I want? Or do I let go and look inside?

Once I've taken a fearless and thorough inventory of the good, the bad, and ugly of any day, I reflect and make a decision to do and be a little bit better tomorrow than I was today.

So far, it seems to be working out pretty freaking good!

It will for you too, if you want to stop being so stressed out all the time.

Chapter 7: Enlightenment

"Enlightenment is a state of perfect knowledge or wisdom, combined with infinite compassion."
Matthieu Ricard, Buddhist Monk

The fulcrum for change is predicated on three keys: *decisiveness, motivation, and action.* And, as the quote above suggests, perfect knowledge and wisdom are products of acts of loving kindness, not constructs or theories of the mind.

In other words, enlightenment is verb as well as a state of being.

It is realized through action, conscious or not. Enlightenment is also a product of choice: doing or not doing. To love or hate. To be kind or spiteful. Accepting or resentful.

Each attitude, action, or response to a given thought, person, or situation informs our understanding of what is and how we feel. This relational and experiential wisdom is what makes us enlightened beings. Books can't create it. Lectures and seminars can't make us enlightened. *The only path to enlightenment is through.* Being still enough to pay attention to what is. As such, *enlightenment is a visceral experience which never leaves us.*

Once we have become enlightened, we can't erase that internal wisdom.

In short, *enlightenment is knowing.*

Enlightenment vs. The Enlightenment

The focus of this chapter is on the process of enlightenment for individuals, not necessarily systems, cultures, or groups. However, as individuals nurture their innate need for love and acceptance and for connection and unity, the natural by-product is enlightenment. And in that sense, a paradigm shift similar to the period historians refer to as "The Enlightenment" is regaining favor in many circles.

What was the Enlightenment?

According to an article published on the Council for Foreign Relations website dated, February 17, 2023, entitled, "What Is the Enlightenment and How Did It Transform Politics?"

education.cfr.org/learn/reading/what-enlightenment-and-how-did-it-transform-politics

"The Enlightenment was an intellectual movement in the seventeenth and eighteenth centuries that sought to improve society through fact-based reason and inquiry. The Enlightenment brought secular thought to Europe and reshaped the ways people understood issues such as liberty, equality, and individual rights. Today those ideas serve as the cornerstone of the world's strongest democracies."

There were basically five influential ideas from the Enlightenment:

1. Opposition to Absolute Monarchy: No ruler should have absolute power
2. Separation of Powers: Power should be distributed across different branches of government
3. Liberty and Individual Rights: All men (people) possess natural rights to life, liberty, and property
4. Equality: All men (people) are created equal and no one should be born into more power than another
5. Free-Market Capitalism: Governments should allow markets to operate with minimal regulations

What does this look like today?

Many of the world's strongest democracies actively support liberty, equality, and individual rights through their laws, customs, and culture. However, there are many societies, mostly authoritarian governments, that actively reject some or most of the Enlightenment's foundational principles.

This begs the question: What can we, individually and collectively, do to honor the constitutional principles and values of *this* country and other cultures abroad, *without sacrificing the liberty of ourselves or others?*

In other words, **how can we lead by example?**

Consider these self-awareness questions:

How are we doing? As a nation? As parents? CEOs? Mangers? Elected officials? Educators? What can we do to be better humans?

Before we can answer these, you may want to revisit chapter six and review the sections about honesty. Also don't forget to check your motives, before you say or do something you may later regret. I recommend taking a page out of Rumi's book regarding the three gates of speech asking ourselves these three critical questions:

Is it true?
Is it necessary?
Is it kind ?

And, I would add, as others have also noted, *is it helpful?*

This simple pause—*a check-up from the neck up*—before we open our mouths or create plans of action, will go a long way toward reducing animosity, vitriol, and hate. And, *with mindful and intentional restraint of pen and tongue, will begin to cultivate cultures of peace and unity rather than division and contempt.*

What is Enlightenment?

Enlightenment is a concept of increasing awareness and knowledge about ourselves and our connection to others. For centuries, it has been explored and sought after by many different cultures and religious traditions throughout history. From Christianity and Islam, Buddhism and Hinduism, to the world's great religions, enlightenment seeks and offers a path towards a deeper understanding of oneself and the world around us. These religious or nontheistic values, codes of conduct, or doctrines teach us to look beyond our everyday concerns and find inner peace, wisdom and inner happiness.

More succinctly, enlightenment is a primary goal of this book.

Before we go further, let's look at a few specific definitions of enlightenment.

The Britannica Dictionary defines enlightenment as:

1. the state of having knowledge or understanding; awareness.
2. *the Enlightenment*: a movement of the 18th century that stressed the belief that science and logic give people more knowledge and understanding than tradition and religion
3. *Buddhism*: a final spiritual state marked by the absence of desire or suffering

According to Websters Dictionary, Buddhism is a final blessed state *marked by the absence of desire or suffering. To want no more.*

For me, enlightenment is a state of being, not a destination. It's about being fully aware and present. *Enlightenment is freedom from the bondage of self.*

Having goals for personal improvement are not "bad." Our struggle comes in the striving. In our attachment to specific outcomes or expectations. Or when we attach our identity to possessions or status. These are anchors that inhibit our ability to inhabit the space between extremes. For example, the gravity and weight of greed and our unquenchable desire for more which keep us stuck.

Until we learn how to detach and fully surrender, we will never be truly free.

Freedom can only come through enlightenment and complete surrender. I know this from thirty-eight plus years of recovery. Perhaps that is why it remains so elusive. Our need for certainty are shackles of an unenlightened soul.

And sadly, too often, the magnetic pull of our ego and pride are so great that we refuse to believe we can be free without control.

Guess what, the earth will continue to orbit the sun with or without your help.

The waves will continue to rise and fall just as the sun and moon will always set and rise.

Our obsession with control and propensity to say, "I got this" as I mentioned earlier, stand in the way of our freedom. This illusion of power and control stands between us and enlightenment.

To be free, we must quit trying to play God.

It's worth noting that there is no one set answer to the question: *how do I become enlightened?* This is a deeply personal quest best left for you to discover on your own.

The Ultimate Goal of Buddhism is Enlightenment

The goal of Buddhism is to become enlightened and reach nirvana. Nirvana is believed to be attainable only with the *elimination of all greed, hatred, and ignorance* within a person. Nirvana signifies the end of the cycle of death and rebirth.

Enlightenment means to become a Buddha—the pinnacle of human development and potential—and it is the ultimate aim in Buddhism. It is something that every single being on earth has the potential to achieve.

Right now, we're not Buddhas—instead, we experience a life full of problems and constant ups and downs. We act in ways we think will bring us true happiness, but all too frequently they only result in heartache, pain, or misery. Take greed or lust for example. Does fulfilment of desire for more ever create lasting peace?

No.

At best, we may make more money or have a bigger home, but greed is greed and by definition, is never satisfied.

Lust is the precursor to greed and like greed, is never satisfied. And being bombarded with marketing and advertising messages or facing self-esteem issues of not quite measuring up to the Joneses, only perpetuates our perceived gap of not having enough and triggers our insatiable appetites for more.

Sex sells. So do emotional appeals for more money, higher status, new clothes, new looks, better looks, etc. But no matter how much we already may have; it rarely feels like it's enough.

Trust me, as a recovered alcoholic and drug addict I know a lot about lust and greed and always wanting more. When it comes to drinking, "one is too many and a thousand, never enough." The same can be said for hundreds of other unhealthy obsessive-compulsive disorders.

So how do we escape the life-sucking vortex of more?

The short answer is that it's a process. And enlightenment is an integral part of that process, one I am still learning and exploring.

In a <u>blog</u> entitled, "How Do The World's Great Religions Teach the Path to Enlightenment?," *(backpackbuddha.com/ blogs/ enlightenment/ the-journey-to-enlightenment-how-the-worlds-great-religions-teach-the-path-to-inner-peace-and-spiritual-awakening)* Leif Harum offers a brief outline of what enlightenment means to several major religions. six of them are paraphrased below.

In Hinduism the concept of enlightenment is based on total awareness of a situation, in terms of the physical and spiritual centers of the body. Known as "Moksha" to Hindus, enlightenment is a state of liberation from the cycle of reincarnation and union with the ultimate reality. This path to enlightenment involves following the Four Purusharthas which are: Dharma (*duty*), Artha (*material wealth*), Kama (*pleasures*), and Moksha (*spiritual liberation*). The path also includes yoga, meditation, devotion, study of scripture and service to others. It's understood that the ultimate goal of these practices is to transcend the ego and realize one's true nature as part of the ultimate reality or Brahman.

In Jainism The path to enlightenment is known as "Nirvana" or "Kaivalya" and is described as the state of being free from the cycle of reincarnation. Jainism's path is based on the Ratnatraya or "three Gems": samyagdarśana (*correct perception*), samyagjñāna (*right* *knowledge*), and samyakchāritra (*right conduct*). Together these constitute the mokṣamarga or the path to liberation. *Jainism emphasizes non-violence, non-attachment and self-control as essential steps towards spiritual advancement.* The ideal goal is to attain spiritual liberation by purifying the soul and *ultimately attaining a state of perfect knowledge, vision, conduct and power.*

In Sikhism enlightenment is a spiritual state known as "Mukti," that can be achieved through a combination of *ethical living, divine grace, and regular spiritual practices including meditation and prayer.* Sikhs believe that the ultimate goal of human life is to merge with the ultimate reality, or God. *The focus is on living a virtuous life, based on the principles of love, devotion and self-surrender, and ultimately to transcend the ego and realize one's unity with God.*

In Christianity enlightenment is referred to as "Salvation" or "Union with God" and is described as the state of being saved from sin and eternal death and gaining eternal life in heaven. Enlightenment hinges on the belief in the ultimate sacrifice—Jesus' death on the cross and resurrection—as the forgiveness of all sin. The Christian path to enlightenment involves developing a personal relationship with God through faith in Jesus Christ. *Christians believe that by following the teachings of Jesus, living a virtuous life, and embracing a life based on love, they can achieve salvation and eternal life with God.*

In Islam enlightenment is referred to as "Tawheed" or "Oneness" and is described as the state of knowing and experiencing the unity of God. Some say that Islamic enlightenment is a combination of reason and religion, and that Islam does not require the same conflict between science and religion as Christianity. The Islamic path to enlightenment involves the *submission to the will of God* and *adherence to the Five Pillars of Islam*: the declaration of *faith, prayer, fasting,* giving to *charity,* and *pilgrimage to Mecca. Muslims believe that by following the teachings of the Quran and the example of the Prophet Muhammad, they can achieve a deep understanding of the unity of God and ultimately reach a state of spiritual enlightenment.*

In Judaism enlightenment is referred to as "Devekut" and is described as the state of spiritual attachment to God. The Jewish path to enlightenment involves the study of the Torah, performing mitzvot, and engaging in prayer and meditation. Through these practices, Jews believe they can achieve a deeper understanding of God and ultimately reach a state of spiritual enlightenment and connection to God.

In summary, there are a multitude of religious and non-religious practices of becoming enlightened. None is necessarily better than another, however, **most have**

one thing in common: a willingness and desire to build a relationship with a spiritual power greater than ourselves. Often this is manifested in various forms or prayer or meditation and may include a variety of other customs, rituals, or practices.

The ultimate goal of enlightenment is not an arrival. It is to build a relationship with divine spiritual force and live lives based on compassion, kindness, unity and love.

In short, **enlightenment is about union**. To become one with the *common thread of energy that connects all things.*

Some refer to this energy as God, Spirit, Collective Consciousness, Gus (Great Universal Spirit), The Universe, God Consciousness, "Higher Power," etc.

According to a 2012 Pew Research study (www.pewresearch.org/religion/2012/12/18/global-religious-landscape-exec), 85% of humans around the world identify with some type of religion and many others have some form of spiritual beliefs. Whether religious, spiritual, agnostic, or atheist, I am sure we can all agree that there are forces in nature and the world around us that neither we nor science can fully explain or put a label on.

We don't need to.

Labels are quite simply a tool for connection and communication. And they can also be used as weapons as with wars over ideology, prevailing political parties, or governance of nations.

The point is not what we call this energy so much as what we can do to better understand it so we may in turn *improve our lives and relationships; to be more compassionate with ourselves and each other.*

Recognizing, acknowledging, and accepting that this unseen force is real may not be easy for many. The purpose of spiritual enlightenment is to open our eyes and hearts and minds and souls to levels of compassion and presence beyond comprehension of our conscious, ego-driven minds. And later, as we will explore in the next chapter, to continue to achieve new levels of spiritual awakening, personal growth, and relational intimacy.

Enlightenment can't be taught; it can only be realized through self-discovery and self-realization. There is no one set example of what enlightenment looks or feels like. It is something unique that can only be described by those who have become enlightened beings.

Lastly, nearly all religions mention the surrender of ego or the self as a prerequisite for enlightenment.

How are *you* doing so far?

Chapter 8: Spiritual Awakening

"Now faith is confidence in what we hope for and assurance about what we do not see."
Hebrews 11:1 NIV

The sacred pre-dawn hours, before the birds awake or the sun begins to rise, is when I feel most connected to the spiritual essence. Here is where I feel the heartbeat of *my* soul—*our* soul—pulsing within. The unseen, uncertain, but essential energy that connects us all.

These are times when I feel most fully present, awake, and alive.

Sometimes in the stillness I hear gentle whispers:

"Today's gonna be a great day." And "Keep going." Or "Trust me, I'll show you what to do next."

On occasion, my first thoughts are not full of joy or gratitude. Instead, my private time is rudely interrupted by a talking monkey in a clown suit that tries to steal my joy, smacking cymbals and grunting comments that are not kind: "You should be further along than you are right now at this stage of your life." "Do you really think you have what it takes to_____?"

Or worse, "You suck!"

When I hear that monkey, I won't lie, sometimes I listen and believe what it says.

But today it's quiet. And I don't plan to rattle its cage.

Right now, the only voice I hear is the one that says, "I love you and everything is as it should be in *this moment*. Now follow through with the plans I've laid on your heart and make it a great day."

And to that, I look to the still dark sky and simply say, "Thank you."

This is yet one of a hundred thousand moments unmarred by the worries yet to sneak into my brain, or the plans I've made or am following.

Sometimes I second-guess my choice, wondering if this is the correct path. A path to what? To where? I don't know unless I am on it.

Therein lies the problem for so many of us: we are never certain that the choices we've made or the road we've taken will lead us to where we want to go—*unless we completely let go.*

There are an infinite number of paths to awakening and enlightenment. Many are found in the midst of pain or suffering. It has been my experience that the greatest breakthroughs in my life happen after I've learned a lesson that ends the suffering.

This is what I described earlier about the compulsion to drink being removed. It wasn't until I was hurting bad enough that I became open to the possibility of a different path forward. This and moments like it are what I call awakenings. We all have them.

What exactly is a spiritual awakening and how does it compare to enlightenment?

A spiritual awakening is a process of personal transformation that involves a shift in consciousness and worldview. It can also be called enlightenment, bliss, or discovering nirvana. There is no one clear-cut definition that all agree on.

Simply put, any time you realize or accept something important and life-changing, it can be called an awakening, because it's almost like you were asleep before.

If you've ever had an "ah-ha moment" or deep and profound insights, these too, are forms of awakening. Manifestations made real. Awakenings may or may not be spiritual in nature. I'll leave that up to you to discern.

On a personal level, I've already shared some facets of my spiritual awakening though my recovery journey: The third step miracle with my sponsor. The cathartic healing with my therapist, and many more inexplicable and transformational moments and miracles that would take a whole book to share.

My spiritual awakenings for the most part have been of the "educational variety."

I've spent countless hours and thousands of dollars trying to find some magic formula or panacea that would take away all my doubts, worries, fears, and insecurities. As empowering as external motivation, will power and self-help, or spiritual enlightenment can be, by themselves, they are not enough to sustain lasting transformation. To overcome my shortcomings, real or perceived, and to feel more confident, I needed something more.

But what?

First, I needed to become more self-aware and to know what would motivate me to become willing to change. Second, to face my fears and insecurities, I needed courage. Third, I needed a plan. Last, I needed to work that plan.

If I was to break free, especially from my addiction, it was necessary for me to take personal responsibility for my own growth but not rely completely on self-will. It was highly recommended that I find someone to guide me (a sponsor). I had to humble myself enough to not only admit that I had a problem but also be vulnerable enough to ask for help. I followed the suggestions which ultimately led me to a mental, physical, and spiritual awakening and long-term sobriety.

In recovery, I found a spiritual solution to my mental and physical problem—I came to believe in a power greater than myself, which I call God or Higher Power (HP).

Ultimately, this spiritual awakening moved me from a perpetual state of fear and addiction, to freedom and recovery.

Chapter 9: Grace

"It is finished."
Jesus

Have you ever had this thought:

If "It is finished," why do I still feel like shit?

I have, thousands of times.

Why?

Why do we feel guilty when we fall short? Or full of shame when we don't feel like we measure up? Or continue to gossip or judge others who are different than us?

I don't know.

And I no longer wear the Christian label, not that that matters anyway.

I wore it for twenty plus years and learned a few things. Foremost, that the entire Christian religion hinges on one thing: Jesus' death and resurrection; the belief that what the Bible says actually happened.

Even if it cannot be proven beyond a reasonable doubt, the entire Christian doctrine is built upon the "fact" that Jesus died as atonement for our sins and, according to scripture, rose again.

Full stop.

Whether you believe that or not, it is a perfect example of grace, love, and forgiveness all wrapped up into one tidy sequence of events.

But life isn't that easy, is it?

Why?

If one unequivocally believes in the imperatives of Christianity, why then, even after Jesus paid the ultimate price of "our" supposed sins by being speared to death and nailed to a wooden cross, do so many still fail to believe in grace?

Why do so many, whether Christian or not, choose to coddle their shortcomings or hide or deny them, thereby creating guilt or shame and not make a healthier decision to flip the script on "sin" and look to the light within?

I don't know.

Maybe because making mistakes isn't as bad as we think. They make us human, not sinners, broken, or damaged.

Perhaps it's because, regardless of religious upbringing or not, we've been fed a steady diet of do's and don'ts, commandments and rules, disguised as "law" and have chosen to believe that our value and worth are wholly predicated on being perfect. That if we're anything less than perfect, we will be condemned.

Bullshit.

Who's to say that what is right for you is right for me?

Besides, the world is full of imperfect people, religious or spiritual or not, doing the best they can with what they have. Some strive to be better. Others are perfectly content to be as they are.

Either way it is not for us to judge or condemn them. How others live is not our concern, especially if we refuse to look at our own reflection in the mirror first.

Rigorous and honest self-reflection and taking personal responsibility for our own attitudes and actions is tantamount to our own personal growth and emotional maturity. Blaming or shaming others or refusing to have the courage to face our own shortcomings, is foolish and hypocritical.

I don't want to be a hypocrite, yet there are times when I am.

I am a work in progress.

My point is this: Let us pursue our own paths, spiritual or not, and mind our own freaking business. This could be the secret sauce to creating lasting world peace.

Suffering is Inevitable. Fear is Optional.

Scores of religions explore a pathway to peace, an end of suffering, of pain, of guilt and shame. As discussed earlier, most of these "rules" or codes of moral conduct are guides to some form of spiritual awakening or enlightenment.

Suffering is the first noble truth in Buddhism. It is the pathway to peace. But who likes to suffer? I don't know about you but I don't wake up in the morning and say, *Hey, I can't wait to suffer today!*

Not all suffering is tied to guilt or shame. A lot of it is, but it doesn't need to be.

Just because we mess up doesn't mean we are bad, less than, or unworthy. Nor does it mean we're going to hell, as some would lead you to believe.

Conversely, according to the Bible, God's spirit lives inside every one of us who choose to believe. According to Jesus, it's always been there, whether we believe or not, *because God loves all of us, not just the righteous right or liberal left*. Not only the wealthy but the poor and desperate, and especially foreigners and those in need.

He also said that we could do all the same things that he did—walk on water, heal the sick, etc., *if* we tapped into the spirit of God that already exists inside.

So, the real question, whether Christian or not, is *do we believe in grace and miracles?*

If "It is finished" and if we already have that which we seek, why are we still suffering?

What's in our way?

Fear? Doubt? Lack of belief, trust, faith? Pride? Ego?

I'll leave that for you to wrestle with.

Now, let's look at grace. What is it? Grace is unmerited favor. It's about *acceptance, not obedience.* Yet all too often we confuse the two. Grace is a term with religious connotation but it's not religious.

One might wonder, is the Bible simply a book of allegories to make us feel good when we obey or to lay a guilt trip on us so we feel like shit when we're disobedient.

Does this mean that if we do not fully trust or believe or act in a kinder more compassionate way towards ourselves or others, that we're going to hell?

It may, if you believe it to be so. But again, grace replaces such nonsense.

I'll leave that for you to figure out.

Regardless of our religious or non-religious and spiritual beliefs, are we doomed to a life of suffering? Some say so. Others unequivocally believe in concepts of grace, or love, or forgiveness or all of these. Some fully embrace the concept of God's magic eraser of grace as outlined in the new testament. Others don't.

As mentioned earlier, I had to learn to accept grace and the love of others before I could relearn how to love myself.

Recovering from addiction and alcoholism—the outward manifestations of an internal condition of self-centered fear—depends on grace, and love, and action.

All of it.

In recovery, I learned that a life run by self-will without some form of a moral code or spiritual barometer is a life ruled by fear, not grace and certainly not love.

When we operate out of fear and self-will, happiness will continue to elude us. Resistance to change for some, especially those with a predisposition of obsessive or compulsive behavior, can be deadly.

But this is not a hopeless situation. Surrender and grace make healing possible. So does effort.

When we swallow our pride and loosen our white-knuckled grip on the past, letting go of fear, anger, resentments, and our habitual propensity to incessantly worry about the future, then and only then will we begin to truly heal.

In other words, we will continue to suffer until we learn to embrace the present, *here, now always* because that's all there is anyway. Everything else is a memory or a mirage. Grace is like a Tide pen; we know the stain is there but grace removes it.

When we learn to listen to the voice of God inside (whatever that sounds like to you) and learn to trust ourselves more, our suffering will subside. And when we learn what our pain or suffering is trying to teach us, it will "magically" disappear.

The concept of grace, like forgiveness, is rooted in love. We'll explore love in the next chapter, but for now, I want to share two stories of grace to further illustrate the concept and then leave the rest up to you to discover on your own.

I have had more miracles happen in my life that had little or nothing to do with personal effort. For example, the "God shot" I had at the bottom of that hill before staggering into my first recovery meeting was a moment of grace that planted the seed of hope that I could get and stay sober.

After a drunken accident that nearly cost me my right hand, I had come home from college with good intentions to stop drinking. I was only 21. And my life was slipping away.

After closing the bars yet again, I came out of a blackout, head hung low, shuffling along a gravel path atop a ridge, just before dawn.

I saw a hill lit by morning sun and stepped onto it not realizing it was covered in dew. The next thing I remember, I was tumbling head over heels before landing on my butt at the bottom of that hill.

Head between my knees, picking at stickers on my oversized thrift store suit, I cried out, "God please help me! Help me stop drinking, I'm too young to die."

In that moment, I recalled from a meeting schedule one of my brother's friends had left on our coffee table, that there was a meeting not far from where I was...

In that moment of desperation, I found the courage to follow God's prompting and went to my first recovery meeting.

It was a start. But I wasn't done, yet.

Eventually the pain of continuing to try to control my drinking on my own (self-will) wasn't working

In desperation and out of fear of dying, I made the decision to check into rehab. It wasn't until I accepted the love and grace of others to help me recover and started to practice the steps that my life really began to change.

Over time, I have learned that the secret to happiness is to embrace grace and find the courage to change.

Success requires both.

And, as many in recovery say, *faith without works is dead.*

Even if you don't believe in miracles or "divine intervention" consider another true story from my memoir, *Beyond Recovery.*

While starting a family was something we both wanted, there were also some very real fears that surfaced when the pregnancy test came back positive. A few members of my first wife's family had medical issues that had the possibility of showing up in our unborn child. Her sister had been diagnosed with a bipolar disorder and her brother was born with cerebral palsy and is deaf. To assuage our anxiety, she had a series of tests done.

The doctors concluded that there should be no cause for concern related to any potential hereditary issues. Regardless, we still discussed the "what ifs," and both agreed that no matter what, we would love the child and provide as best we could. We were not going to church, though she was raised Catholic, but we prayed anyway and trusted that all would be well.

As young future parents we were flat broke and worried about food, day care, clothes, and all the usual. But friends came through and we always had enough.

All was going well until she started having pre-term contractions at seven and a half months. We feared that she'd miscarry. Her doctor ordered her to bed rest for the next six weeks. She was to take it easy and not do anything strenuous. In a subsequent follow up, it was determined that the baby was breached and that he wanted her to stay on bed rest. We were to come back in a week to see if the baby would turn on its own.

A week later, we were back at Marin General Hospital. She was admitted and given a private room where we waited for the doctor to arrive. He was a kind man with a gentle bedside manner that put us at ease. He put some jelly on her belly and scanned with the ultrasound. You could see a tiny silhouette of our baby inside. The heart monitor beat steadily and made a loud whooshing sound.

"This won't hurt, but you will feel some pressure," he explained, pressing firmly on her abdomen in a counter-clockwise motion. After a few minutes he had successfully turned our baby head side down.

"That should be good," he said. "But I want you to stay for a bit while we monitor you and the baby. I'll be back in an hour to see if we can send you home." We sighed in relief.

I pulled a chair alongside her bed so we could chat while we waited. She scooted up in her bed, as she did,

I heard the heart monitor slow. My own heart dropped—I felt like I just got punched in the gut. I had already been down this road with my grandmother a few years earlier. I didn't want to relive this. Not now. Not with our unborn baby.

"Did you hear that?" I asked, heart pounding in my chest, worried about our baby.

"No. What?"

"When you moved, the baby's heart slowed." I said, pointing to the ultrasound.

"I didn't hear anything." Adele replied, shaking her head.

The baby's heart went back to normal as she sat still. My mind was reeling. I had a knot in my stomach.

"Do you think it's possible that the umbilical cord is pinched? Maybe it got wrapped around the baby's neck when the doctor turned it?" She looked at me like I was overreacting.

"I think it's fine. He knows what he's doing," she said, not overly concerned.

"What if you go home and you bend over to pick up a bar of soap in the shower and the baby dies?" I worried. "Can you do me a favor—get out of bed and bend at the waist to touch your toes?"

"Fine." She said, rolling her eyes.

She sat up, and slid to the edge of the bed, got to her feet, and bent over to touch her toes. As soon as she did, an alarm screeched on the ultrasound—the baby's heart slowed to near flat line.

"Nurse!" I shouted, then turned to Adele. "Stand up and see if that helps."

As soon as she stood up, the baby's heart came back to a normal rhythm.

"Nurse, we need the doctor back here, now!"

I was climbing the walls, consumed by fear of losing our baby. The nurse arrived and we told her what happened. I demanded to get the doctor back.

Twenty minutes later, the doctor arrived. He concurred that the cord may be pinched and decided to do an emergency C-section. He explained everything in great detail, not at all rattled by the situation. He said that she and the baby would be fine, and that he needed to clear an OR and would get back to us shortly.

He returned and said we were scheduled for surgery in forty minutes. He explained that once Adele was prepped, the procedure would only take seven and a half minutes. In the meantime, he suggested we call her parents if they wanted to be here. I called and told Phyllis what was going on. They lived nearby and showed up just before we left for the OR.

I could see the fear on Adele's face.

The clock ticked slowly as we waited. Finally, the doctor came to get us. Her expression softened, but I could still see the apprehension in her eyes as the doctor wheeled Adele off to surgery. As he whisked past me, he told me to put on scrubs and a mask and said the nurse would come get me in a couple minutes.

The nurse returned as he promised. Seven and a half minutes later, our son was born.

He looked so tiny and wrinkled as the nurse help him up. I flashed a nervous smile, holding my breath as I waited for him to cry. Finally, after what seemed like an eternity, he let out a loud cry.

Our son was alive! We were new parents.

It was and is one of the happiest moments of my life. From the fear of possibly losing him to the pure joy of his first cry, I was overwhelmed with gratitude.

The nurse cleaned him up and wrapped him in a receiving blanket. I held him close to Adele's face. " He smells so good!" she glowed, kissing our newborn son, Andrew on the cheek.

I was beaming. I went to introduce Andrew to my in-laws, John and Phyllis before returning him to the nurse to stay in the nursery while Adele was moved to the recovery room down the hall.

I couldn't wait to show Andrew off to his Grandparents.

Phyllis was always a strong woman who I never saw cry. As she held my son, she was overcome with joy, tears rolling off her pale cheeks. John beamed as he held Andrew carefully before handing him back to me.

Pay Attention to the Universal Prompts & Embrace Grace

"…Have your wife bend over and touch her toes to see if the baby's heart slows."

Had I not listened and acted upon that thought, our son may not have survived.

Here are the facts: Grace is real. Love is real. And miracles happen every day. Some of us are fortunate enough to know first-hand how powerful they can be.

Chapter 10: Love

"Be completely humble and gentle; be patient, bearing with one another in love."
Ephesians 4:2 NIV

Why do I need a chapter on love? Because it is the most important thing in the world and sadly, the world could use a little more love.

Perhaps you could too.

Before the final results of the 2024 election were in, I posted this on Facebook before going to bed:

Love cannot be bought, has no political affiliation and is not subject to influence by corporate or special interests.

Love will always prevail if we honor it and share it for good. And the opposite can be said of hate. Today, I choose to love even when it's far easier to hate.

The next morning, after reading many articles and opinions on the New York Times and seeing that Trump had won the election and that the senate was controlled by Republicans, and likely the house as well I added this comment:

Love is also the foundation of my prevailing mission and purpose for the rest of my life.

Love is a cause worth fighting for. A cause worth embracing.

Love is a fundamental, universal, inarguable, liberating, unquestionable, and spirit-driven principle that changes lives.

My prayer for all humanity is this:
Learn to Lead with Love.

Learn to Lead with Love

This is my prayer for all humanity. This is what I want for the world. This is what I believe in my heart of hearts. To me, love is the deep-seated spiritual energy that resides in each and every one of us. It has a thousand faces for us to connect with each other and not fight over. And yet we continue to fight and hate and judge others different from us.

How sad.

What's the solution?

We must learn to lead with love.

Our fight for righteousness and uniqueness sadly and all too often, is not loving. Rather it's hateful, spiteful, divisive, and not loving or kind. Nor is it spiritual.

The results of our quest to be right and therefore to judge others who do not share our opinions is wrong and often driven by self-centered fear, not love.

From Jihad to Jesus and everything in-between the holy war and insidious fight for righteousness is literally killing us! **If we ever hope to have peace, we must cease fighting everyone and everything we disagree with.** If we are to be truly free and survive as a species, we must learn to accept our differences and **love everybody always.**

This is simple, but not easy.

I too, have judgmental, selfish, and self-centered tendencies. But awareness is not a solution. Surrender and effort are.

As a recovered alcoholic I know the solution for me is a spiritual one, yet I flirt with self-will all the time because, like you, I am human, perfectly imperfect.

So, what does this have to do with love, the golden rule, or kindness?

Everything.

I must be kind to myself because if I'm not, you will know. My shitty attitude will show. When I'm not centered or choose to consciously or unconsciously operate from selfish ambition—my way or the highway— my days suck.

However, when I return to center, grounded and focused on love, and do what I can to lead with love, my days are pretty freaking stellar and chill.

"Those who love peace must learn to organize as effectively as those who love war."
~Martin Luther King Jr.

To counteract our insidious propensity and proclivity of distrust and hate, we must learn to love ourselves and each other.

It starts with empathy and compassion; with understanding and listening and not trying to fix or control other peoples' problems, especially our husbands, wives, or other family members!

We must learn to mind our own fucking business and also not be shy about what we value.

However, anything and everything we do must come from a place of love and forgiveness not condemnation, judgement, and hate!

"Do everything in love."
1 Corinthians 16:14 NIV

The great fact is this: *without love, we have nothing.*

With few exceptions, we know how to give and receive love. The problem is sometimes we lose sight of what we already have and, in our self-absorbed small worlds, forget to extend love to ourselves or others.

Love is much more than a feeling. It's power is undeniable. Love is an act of the deepest and kindest form of compassion we can give to ourselves and another. Love is the source of all motivation and inspiration.

Power Pause, Peace

Please take a moment right now to text or call a family member or someone significant in your life and let them know how much you love them.

I cannot stress this enough. I recently had a dear friend lose their son in a car crash. Nothing anyone says or does will bring him back.

We can never say "I love you" too much.

We must also love (not like) our enemies, though we may despise who they are or what they do we do not have to condone or like their behavior, but we must love everybody always.

Why?

Because we are all connected and to hate of another is actually a condemnation of ourselves. Besides, when we carry hate in our hearts, the person we despise is rarely aware of how we feel and therefore do not suffer. To the precise extent that we harbor hatred or malice toward others, we suffer gravely.

It's been said that holding resentment or anger toward another is like giving them free rent in our head. If we want to be free, we must learn to let that shit go and embrace love. To use the words of Jack Kornfield, we must surround them in "lovingkindness."

We'll explore this more in the next chapter on forgiveness, but for now, please pause, rub your hands to together and raise them up.

Feel the warmth of your palms as you touch your fingertips to the crown of your head, your third-eye, your throat, your heart, your solar plexus, your groin, and the tips of your toes.

Feel the energy rise, creating a warm glow from the soles of your feet to the top of your head, and let it flow. Feel the energy rushing through your blood, to every cell, muscle, and bone of your body.

Now take a deep breath and hold it for a count of four.

Then, exhale. And feel any and all negative energy rushing out like a drain and take one more deep breath. Feel the light inside you pulse as your heart beats slower.

Exhale and give yourself a big hug. Feel the corners of your mouth turn upward to the sky and smile knowing you are not only loved, but you are also alive.

For me, the secret of being a good human, to yourself and others is **one word: LOVE.**

"Do unto others as you would have them do unto you."-
Matthew 7:12
Or straight from Jesus: "Love one another," and "Love your
neighbor as yourself."

Even if we know it's right to love each other, why is it hard to love those we don't like or who are different from us. Why do we try to control those around us to be like us? To believe what we believe?

I don't know but we all do it.

Such behavior isn't healthy nor does it foster stronger relationships.

There is great wisdom in the Al-Anon creed, "I didn't cause it, I can't control it, and I can't cure it." We may want to become more curious in our relationships and ask ourselves, *what can I learn by listening to the opinions of others?* Am I willing to hear why their beliefs are important to them? Or am I convinced that my opinions are the only ones that really matter and therefore everyone else is wrong?

How can we learn to keep our mouths shut when the opinions of others do not align with our own beliefs? What can we learn by listening and not trying to convince everyone to be like us?

If our role or goal is to build communities based on love, trust, humility, compassion, and kindness doesn't it make logical sense that we must hear the voices of many, not one?

If we are to succeed at building unity and supportive communities and cultures, we must learn to embrace the space between left and right, right or wrong, and instead become more curious about what is not on one extreme or the other.

We must find the point of equilibrium and once discovered, return to it more and more frequently. As we do, we will discover peace and joy that otherwise will continue to elude us.

The only condition to finding the happiness of balance and joy and of being grounded in mind, body, spirit and relationships are these: *we must do all of it with love and we must believe in the possibility of peace.*

Chapter 11: Forgiveness

"If we really want to love, we must learn how to forgive."
Mother Theresa

Resentments are toxic and can be deadly.

In some respects, I wish that there was no trauma in my own past.

There is.

As previously mentioned, for years I carried the anger of my father leaving us. Though I did my best to make ninth step amends to him several times before his passing, my unresolved pain and anger continued to linger beneath the surface. When I was stressed out, it would rear its ugly head as yelling or wanting to break shit, especially glass.

To snap this insidious cycle of anger and self-destructive behavior, I had to find healthy ways to process my emotions and learn how to forgive others including myself.

I've heard it said that all events which have hurt us leave a hole in our hearts; an emptiness. The holes never fully seem to heal. We may turn to a hundred different things in a vain attempt to take away that agony—to not feel the pain. I'm sure all of us have a measure of regret, or pain from our own past, or know someone who lived through hellish situations. How do we cope? What do we do when our heart is broken or we've lost someone close? At the risk of sounding preachy, I feel compelled to dig a little deeper into this concept of facing our demons—our own Goliaths.

Forgiveness is the bedrock of enlightenment and awakening.

There is great joy in the world, yet there is much heartache and unresolved pain, as well.

For some, the holes make us stronger. We learn to adapt. We learn to forgive ourselves. We learn that bad things can and do happen to good people. For some, like me, we learn to rely on a higher power to carry us through. We surrender and look to a God of our understanding—pick one or none—I believe that of our own human power we are too feeble to overcome any of the deep scars on our own volition.

We need something more.

If we are willing to grow, stretch, and have the courage to face our fears and painful past and then seek help—either from trusted friends, professionals, or community-based support groups—we can change. Ultimately, we can break the chains that bind us. We can drop the rock of old attitudes, beliefs, pains, and hurt. We can, in a word, *forgive*.

This sounds simple in black and white. It is far from it. For many it may never happen. For others it may take a lifetime. It has been my experience, that, in order to break free from the pain of my past, forgiveness is requisite.

We need to **first forgive ourselves, then others**. In so doing, we unlock the shackles that enslave us. One by one we can slowly begin the process of change and healing.

Transformation starts with recognition of what we want to change—something has to be off, or not right for us before we even consider wanting to change. It can be a problem, a habit, behavior, or actions.

Most of that change is mental—thoughts, attitudes, beliefs, values, perceptions, etc. The other part is action and complete surrender.

Faith, willingness, and courage to change are next. Then comes introspection, soul searching, and self-assessment.

Finally, we embark to keep our own houses in order and **apologize when we are wrong**, mindful of how our attitudes and actions affect those around us. *We practice kindness, patience, tolerance, love, and understanding.*

When we make a conscious decision to take personal responsibility and intentionally practice adding value to the lives of others, our entire world changes.

Eventually, those holes that look like pock marks on our soul, become a great source of inspiration for helping others. As we practice living a different way of life, we begin to look up again. No longer staring at our shoes, we can see the light in others. We become less concerned with selfish things and more interested in those around us—those we love.

Love is really all every one of us wants and needs. That's all a child really needs—to know that they are loved. That's all a wife needs—to know she is loved and honored, heard, and respected by her husband. That's all a husband needs—to be loved and validated.

We all share a common goal—our souls cry out for one thing and one thing only, **love.** Ultimately, our past becomes a springboard to catapult us into a life filled with joy, meaning and purpose.

If love is living in forgiveness,
then forgiveness is a master key to set us free.

Chapter 12: Finding Inner Peace

Ho'oponono:
I'm sorry, please forgive me, thank you, I love you.

Ho'oponopono is one of the most complete and germane words I know to encapsulate the theme of this entire book. It is a Hawaiian prayer and mantra that can help with reconciliation, self-love, and healing the self. Essentially it is about returning to harmony, to balance, to inner peace.

Shalom is another rich word packed with meaning, purpose, intention, and healing.

Similar to *Nirvana, Shalom is more than a word, it's a feeling. A state.* Something to embrace and live by and with.

Whether spoken as mantras, meditations, or prayers, or experienced though our actions and attitudes, discovering and cultivating states of inner peace are simple choices we must make if we want to became free of the bondage of self.

Ultimately, these three words: Ho'oponopono, Shalom, and Nirvana, are symbolic language of the heart whose goal is balance, serenity, presence, and inner peace.

Equally important is understanding that this cycle of struggle and inner peace is a natural one. As previously mentioned, unless or until we reach a state of completion or Nirvana, the cycle of struggle and learning will continue. Acknowledging this and accepting my imperfections and faults is a blessing which offers me the chance to learn from my mistakes without adding to an overstuffed bag of guilt and shame from unresolved conflicts I'm still working through.

Admitting our faults or shortcomings is a challenge for most of us. We falsely believe that we must be defect-free, perfect. None of us are perfect and yet all of us are perfectly imperfect as we are.

The insanity happens when we keep thinking we should be something we are not or that we are inadequate. That we must measure up to some societal standard of conduct and status.

That simply isn't true.

Conversely, there are people we all know who seem not to care what "society thinks" about them. Look to our recent Presidential election of a Trump, a 34x convicted felon and his cabinet appointments to see my point. How many are truly qualified to lead their respective Departments? And yet, the Senate hearings continue...

Politics aside, my point is this: People value change and want to be led.

The greater challenge which we can no longer deny is *how can we become better leaders?* To honor our own values and morals and ethics. To be responsible and take control of our own inner peace, serenity, and happiness rather than waiting for someone or something to give it to us. Or the flipside, to stop blaming others for not giving us what we have failed to give ourselves.

If you want to be happier, be bolder and learn to lead with love more.

For me, the Serenity Prayer is one of the most effective daily reminders and spot-check tools I can use to maintain my own inner peace and serenity. I love it. It's 100% free and can be recited and applied anywhere and at any time to realign my attitude with what my higher power wants. It is has been vital to my sobriety, helping me reclaim or retain my inner peace especially when I feel out of control or consumed by irrational fears.

Here it is:

"God grant me the serenity to accept the things I cannot change, courage to change the things I can, and wisdom to know the difference."
Reinhold Niebuhr

Like the decision to be happy or pursue trains of thought that are positive and not negative, we must also learn to find and embrace the space between if we are to ever find inner peace and serenity. If we ever really want to chill.

Remember what I said earlier: On the other side of the storm are clear skies. Beyond the darkest hours, dawn.

Just because today is raining doesn't mean the sun no longer exists.

Chapter 13: Cultivating Unity and Accepting Diversity

"We must learn to live together as brothers or perish together as fools."
Martin Luther King, Jr.

Nothing inhibits or prevents unity more than judgment and self-righteous indignation.

For the past twelve years headlines have perpetuated a state of fear and division, *an epic battle of Us vs. Them.*

This is not new.

It's been going on for millennia and, sadly, will likely continue until we can learn to love and accept each other as sovereign beings. Until we can be a "kinder, gentler nation."

The recent accelerated polarization of people to one side or another in terms of politics and beliefs, especially in the U.S., to me, is disgusting. Especially when leaders talk a good game but fail to represent what people really want and need. Like more income, lower cost healthcare, affordable housing and education, lower food costs. You know, the basic needs of every human.

For example, the conservative right preaching pro-life when it comes to abortion but having no qualms whatsoever about supplying weapons and killing thousands of innocent civilians in wars in the Ukraine, Israel, Gaza, and elsewhere. Or the left preaching about human rights and aid yet not having enough cajónes to honor international law about war crimes.

Is this unity? Is this compassion?

Where do we balance the rights of others and care for all humans? How do we navigate the tangled web of religion and politics, while also protecting our personal and collective interests? How do we unite people around shared goals and ideas that benefit all not just a few?

How can we feed the 47 million who go to bed hungry every day? Or care for the elderly or allow others who have limited financial resources to get the medical care they need? *How can we change the motives of our healthcare system from profit to prevention?*

How do we leverage our collective intellectual and financial wealth to make this world better for ALL people?

These are questions our leaders should be asking and seeking to resolve. Not what talking points do they need to focus on to win the next election.

Unity is about bridging a gap between our differences.

It's upholding our own constitutional Bill of Rights. It's living by a very simple code of conduct regardless of religious or political beliefs: *compassion, understanding, and courage.*

Why courage?

Because it will take courage and cajónes to make some of the tough decisions for the betterment of many, not just the few. It will take courage to ask questions and seek to understand rather than be understood. It will take courage to accept others who aren't like us. And most of all, to mind our own fucking business when it comes to things that don't concern us like a woman's right to choose, or whom or what we choose to worship.

These are individual constitutional rights and freedoms outlined in the Bill of Rights and our U.S. Constitution. They are the law of the land.

It's been sixty plus years since Martin Luther King marched to promote Civil Rights. Why are we still having conversations about racial inequality, racism, sexism, etc.? Are we really the greatest nation on the planet?

Why, according to 2023 statistics from the *National Alliance to End Homelessness*, did we hit record highs for homelessness with 653,104 people unhoused? Why do 47.4 million people, 13 million children, suffer from food insecurity? How can we justify investing *billions* of dollars in weapons to kill people but not feed or educate or care for our own?

These are the important questions and real problems we face, among many others.

We, the people, want answers, not lip service.

From podium to pulpit, the values and virtues of unity and inclusivity have become hollow promises and propaganda. Sure, many say politically correct things or make claims to appeal to current followers but unless there is follow through with action and a quantifiable, actionable, non-self-serving plan, nothing changes.

I like how my friend Christopher Fairbanks put it, "Freedom and independence require compassion and unification."

Finger pointing and blatant disregard for common decency or decorum have become acceptable. Blame-shifting and fear-mongering have reached epidemic proportions especially during election cycles.

This shit has got to stop.

True unity can only be cultivated from love, not hate.

If we ever hope to me more kind, compassionate or caring, we must start in our own home, in our own places of worship, in our own town, and city, and state. Ultimately unity requires each of us to do our part and not wait for others to do theirs. That's why you need to be bolder.

So, the twenty-trillion-dollar question is how can we solve some or all of these real problems we face collectively as a nation? What and where are the opportunities to connect, grow, or improve?

What are the economic drivers of a healthy economy?

Will increasing tariffs on imports, cutting taxes or other "efficiency cuts actually be more efficient and economically beneficial to most, or just a few? Or will such policies instigate higher inflation and a recession? I can't say, but I doubt this will effectively lower costs and stimulate our economy. We will soon see.

What about plans to eliminate layers of bureaucracy, aka layers of crap?

Yes, we can all agree that government can and should be run more efficiently. Everyone knows that red tape has become a joke not only for businesses, but for those in desperate need of mental health and medical help, or financial aid for college, or food or housing, and much more.

What can we, individually and collectively do that will actually benefit the most people and unite us toward a common goal of better living conditions. Of better wages? Of greater and more affordable options for us to increase our collective intellectual capital? Of lower fuel and food costs? Of affordable housing? Of programs and businesses that prevent addiction (opiate, alcoholism, and all forms of compulsive behaviors) rather than promote or profit from it.

These are the real issues that will bring our consumer-based economy crashing to its knees if not resolved. If people don't have enough money to survive, how in the world will they have enough money to buy other non-essential products and help our economy thrive?

I do not have all the answers.

Perhaps you have a few. If you do, I encourage you to create a plan and implement them. Do your part to make a difference. *Become an agent of positive change not another squeaky wheel or whiner.* The world has enough of those already. And the last time I looked, as my stepfather often said, "There is always plenty of room at the top."

A Call to Action, Not Words

Talking a good game is not indicative of strength or power. Hard work is. Honesty is. Compassion and empathy and understanding are. Asking tougher questions and intentionally becoming more curious and courageous, are paths to unity. Investing time to associate with and get next to those who can make a difference, is a huge step forward along a pathway to peace.

There are endless opportunities for you to put you money and action where your mouth is. One way I do that is by inspiring and helping addicts and alcoholics. By writing books that lift people up and challenging readers to be bolder, and to believe they are capable of so much more.

I encourage you to find a cause greater than yourself and do what you can to bridge a gap—economically, socially, relationally, spiritually, etc. You will not only create stronger connections with people you don't know, but when you serve others and come from a place of compassion and love, you will gain so much more than you could possibly imagine. This is one of the greatest secrets of a great and beautiful life, and it's so simple, and free.

If you want more kindness in the world, **be kinder.**

A Stairway to Heaven or a Highway to Hell?

I don't care which side of the aisle you are on, blame and shame and perpetuating lies or fear isn't a healthy pathway to peace or a *stairway to heaven.* But it is, as the Bible would say, a clear path along a *highway to hell.*

Cultivating unity doesn't mean we have to agree. What it does mean is that we must learn to accept and embrace each other's unique views, cultures, identities, and values, *especially if they are different than our own.*

We must also be honest—do we actually want to create unity and peace?

Or have we become so entrenched in our own values and beliefs that we feel there is no room for others on our bus?

It's not the 1960s folks. Rosa Parks isn't trying to steal your lunch, she only wanted to ride the bus.

It's OK to be politically incorrect. PC is code for saying the right thing to not ruffle feathers, gain supporters, followers, and maintain positional power. Unfortunately, some of the urgency is lost with PC language.

In my opinion, this is a big reason why Trump won again. He defied all odds and, quite frankly, waged one of the greatest comebacks in political history.

How? Why?

Some have theorized that it's because there is a large faction of people who are sick and tired of the pandering and bullshit spewed about from politicians on all sides of the aisles. And that we are hungry for change.

But at what cost?

That's a question far beyond the scope of this book but an important one, nonetheless.

Many want unity and independence. It is possible to have both? **Can we be happy and free?**

Those who figure this out will be the leaders of tomorrow and usher in a new era of unity and peace that the world has yet to see, let alone embrace.

Those that don't, who continue to try tired, old methods and strategies of governance (aka plays of political power and control) will soon become obsolete.

The time will come when the world demands the truth. I believe that one day we will live in harmony but nit until we have learned to embrace and respect our differences. Or share common values. Ironically it is the perpetual uniqueness and common values that bind us tighter.

When we accept this, we will be truly free and we will know peace.

Until then, as long as greed, ego and pride and fear govern our thoughts, attitudes, and beliefs we shall not be free. Nor will we ever experience true unity.

True unity to me is simple: it's to promote and live by a simple rules we already mentioned at the beginning of this book, The golden ones: *Do onto others... Love your neighbor...*

It's also the topic of an excellent book by Bob Goff called, *Everybody Always.*

Here are the cliff notes from Bob's book page on Amazon: Bob teaches you that the path toward the outsized, unfettered, liberated existence we all long for is found in one simple truth: **love people, even the difficult ones, without distinction and without limits.**

Love everybody always. How simple is that?

True Strength Is Not About Being a Bully

Let's take a short detour to the most recent presidential election and a quote from a speech on Nov. 11, 2024, by former president, Barack Obama to 4,500 at the University of Pittsburgh, as reported in the New York Times. He is specifically addressing men in the audience:

"And by the way, I'm sorry, gentlemen, I've noticed this, especially with some men who seem to think Trump's behavior of bullying and putting people down is a sign of strength," he said. "And I am here to tell you that is not what real strength is. It never has been."

"Real strength is about working hard and carrying a heavy load without complaining," he continued, his voice rising into a shout. "Real strength is about taking responsibility for your actions and telling the truth even when it's inconvenient. Real strength is about helping people who need it and standing up for those who can't always stand up for themselves. That is what we should want for our daughters and for our sons, and that is what I want to see in a president of the United States of America."

www.nytimes.com/2024/10/10/us/politics/obama-harris-pittsburgh-democrats.html

Real strength is about getting off our high horses and mucking the fucking barn.

Let's go back to the beginning and my primary motivation for this book. I was raised to be kind. Along the way I became selfish, self-centered, and my behavior created a wave of destruction that nearly cost me my life.

Though I am recovered from the compulsion to drink or do drugs, I still have an ego. And I need to keep it in check.

Every day, upon awakening I have an opportunity, a choice to make about how I want to approach my day. I choose to surrender my will and life over to a power greater than myself on a daily basis. As I do, I become humble. I don't cause harm to others and am a nice guy. When I don't do this, I more apt to be an asshole.

Also, I must continue to check my ego throughout the day. I must not let petty inconveniences or disappointments fester like an unclean wound or my attitude will become infected and smell nasty.

I must be vigilant and not carry grudges. When I am wrong, I must promptly admit it.

When I do these, I don't go to bed angry, I don't wake up with an emotional hangover, and when I pray and turn my will and life of over to my higher power first thing in the morning my days go pretty well.

When I start my day in gratitude rather than stress or worry, my days are good. When I think of the opportunities before me to help clients and others, I am less at risk of drifting into self-will. In other words when I take my eyes off of myself and focus on who I can help, my days are really fucking good.

This starts with my practice. And for you, if you are serious about wanting more peace in your life and your relationships and less stress and discord then you need to do some things differently.

First of all, don't be a dick.

If you think that everyone else must bow down to your whims and ideas, how can you ever hope to build a bridge or connect with others? How can you effectively lead your team, your company or your family if you are stuck in a negative cycle which may be harming you or others?

What's the Secret?

The secret we are seeking lies in compassion not separation or righteousness. As the Dalai Lama says in a *Toward a True Kinship of Faith*s, when we learn to become more curious about others, we can then learn to accept each other and embrace our differences, especially our religions. When we listen, we learn. As we learn, we connect.

This a path to becoming emotionally mature and intelligent.

And rather than building walls to protect our fragile feelings, effectively shutting others out, let's build bridges and become vulnerable enough to let them in.

How hard or scary can that be? Are you up for the challenge?

Chapter 14: Be Grateful, Not Greedy

"Acknowledging the good that you already have in your life is the foundation for all abundance."
-Eckhart Tolle

More, more, more is all about greed, greed, greed, and me, me, me.

Frankly, I find it disgusting, and yet I fall into the more trap just like the Joneses next door.

But life isn't about greed and more money or stuff. It's more than that. It's about relationships.

More will never be enough nor will it make you happy. **It's not all about you.**

Life is dynamic and ever-changing. So are our emotions. Yet we refuse to believe this. Instead, we continue to strive for perfection and certainty, thinking like Goldilocks, that when everything is just right, we will be happy.

But we are never satisfied. We always want more. More money, more time, more love, more respect, more appreciation.

Ironically, it isn't until we stop striving and start looking within, that we find the magic we yearn for.

Gratitude not greed, is the magic key we need to unlock the door to our inner peace and happiness.

Truth is most of us already have more than enough to reach any goal, situation, or ideal state we seek. Whether it's enlightenment, awakening, nirvana, or just having enough money to pay the rent, feed the kids, and put gas in the car, most of us have way more than enough.

The problem is we're greedy and not grateful; we're not satisfied with what we do have. Or perhaps we've forgotten what we do have and are making excuses for all that we don't have rather than finding the courage to work with the tools, skills, resources and talents we do have.

We mistakenly think we need a new strategy, plan, process or some magic pill to give us a shortcut to what we think we want or need.

What we really need is a bigger why. Motivation. A reason to dig deeper.

That motivation starts with becoming grateful for all we already possess.

I firmly believe that *happiness is a state of mind that we can choose*. Ultimately fostering an attitude of gratitude will create the world we want. The inner peace we seek. The connection and unity so necessary to promote a worldview based on similarities not the differences.

I hope and pray that we may seek to find the common ground and celebrate all that makes us different and unique.

Living in a state of gratitude will ensure our personal and collective happiness and will promote world peace.

Some of you may be shaking your heads right now muttering under your breath, I get it Shawn, but I still want more. I want my life to have meaning and purpose, to be significant. And I wanna be a baller. Or at least have more money.

Me too.

So, what are *you* going to do about it?

What's Your Purpose and Calling?

All change requires courage and trust. *As we trust we become free.*

Trusting when we don't know exactly what to do isn't easy, it's scary. It's normal to fear the unknown. But, if we are bold and brave enough to take the first step forward, the answers will come. The path becomes clear as we pay attention to everything and to nothing. As we learn to relinquish our perceived need for certainty and control.

These three: *courage, trust, and action* are the legs which steady our three-legged stool. But here's the paradox: we must do these three and then get out of our own way; we must surrender to the process and powers of the universe to deliver that which we seek. In short, we must do the work and let go of the results. We find joy and peace in the process of doing; the process of being. This is where we discover our purpose.

Why is this so hard?

Because we are obsessed with the need for certainty. We are afraid of making wrong decisions. We pretend to be strong, but behind closed doors we cower and pull the covers over our heads.

Or we go to the other extreme in public and puff ourselves up with pretend power and the illusion of control.

When we live this duplicitous life between extremes we cannot find contentment. Our ego pulls us in multiple directions. We battle beliefs about what we should or shouldn't do, of what we should or shouldn't say, think, or believe.

The result is perpetual struggle.

Sadly, far too many of us allow our inner critics to control who we are and how we act. This is not healthy and, in many manifestations, is sucking the life out of us.

The only way to be free of this inner struggle is to learn to embrace the space that is unknown.

The emptiness between doing and not doing. And to find a way to tap into that limited power within to find what we're searching for.

It is in the space between that we find peace.

It is allowing ourselves to sit and listen in silence, that we hear.

It is in closing our eyes, that we can see and feel and embrace the unknown.

This is where the magic of life lives. It is the seat of our soul, the unlimited energy of all creative energy.

A Wellspring. Our Life Force.

The secret to inner peace is an inside job, driven by humility, courage and gratitude. When we intentionally nurture these, all else seems to flow effortlessly.

Gratitude is a State of Being, Not a Strategy

Contrary to most self-help personal growth books about creating purpose-driven lives, gratitude isn't found in our carefully crafted plans or diligent designs. *Gratitude is lived experience and earned wisdom from all that life teaches us*; from our mistakes and struggles and how we've moved through them.

This may be difficult for you to get your head around especially if you are a planner (or procrastinator), thinker (or overthinker), or leader (or follower), who's been conditioned to believe you must have a strategy in order to succeed. That you must have predictable outcomes from inputs to measure success or growth. That you must line up your ducks before you can proceed.

Bullshit!

While plans are necessary to execute and affect change, the inspiration and clarity we truly need and seek are already inside us.

These precious inspirational gems are found in the endless and continuous stream of collective unconsciousness within us all. They are found by exploring what we already have and know and more importantly, by creating the space to embrace the serendipities of the vast unknown.

Here's the catch: Before we can hear, receive and see, we must first be open, willing, and bold enough to ask and listen, **then patient enough to wait**.

What's "enough"?

Try it and then you'll know.

Confidence comes from practice and experience, not study or theory.

When we release our attachment to certainty, we indirectly invite the unseen forces of the universe to come in. When we stop striving and acknowledge their presence, we are more apt to become inspired. I know that sounds counterintuitive, but it works. The other factor to consider is when we set our intentions higher than anything we could do of our own will and ask a power greater than ourselves to guide us to right thought or action, that's when the magic happens. As we ask then surrender our expectations, the unseen and mystical powers of the universe manifest opportunities for us to grab and take action.

There's an art and science to this.

Remember, confidence comes from practice and experience, not study or theory. That means we must also take action.

Furthermore, mindset matters. When we are in a state of gratitude, we can then catch fleeting glimpses of past, present, and future at once and by doing so become free. Free to think, create, observe, and execute the visions already laid out.

This is much harder to explain than to experience. Those who've taken hallucinogens know exactly what I mean. So too may those who've had near death experiences or been with someone as they are transitioning. Others who practice various forms of prayer and/or meditation also know what this feels like.

When you know, you know.

For the rest of us, we can learn, if we want to.

Those who are looking for more or less or answers will find a path to that which they seek. Those desperately seeking meaning and purpose will find their path when they focus inward.

A Grateful Heart is a Joyful Heart

I am grateful for everything that has happened to bring me to this moment. My life is far greater today than it used to be, and it continues to improve a little bit every day. Your life will improve too, if you want it badly enough and are willing to try something new.

Today, I don't take anything for granted and remain curious to keep becoming a better, more loving, and forgiving human.

Here's a bitter pill you may not be ready to swallow, but it's the truth—our willingness to practice forgiveness is closely tied to our level of gratitude and happiness.

I forgave my dad years ago. But most importantly, I forgave myself.

If you get nothing else from our time together, I hope you learn to have a little more grace, love, and forgiveness for yourself.

I have since learned that humble pie is actually quite tasty.

That does not mean that I had to become a pushover and a "don't-rock-the-boat" or "go-with-the-flow, don't-make-waves" kind of guy.

Far from it. That's not who I am.

But it does mean I need to be more curious and less judgmental or opinionated (I'm still working on that one).

"You, therefore, have no excuse, you who pass judgment on someone else, for at whatever point you judge another, you are condemning yourself, because you who pass judgment do the same things." - Romans 2:1 NIV

It means to build connections and relationships, I need to consider another's viewpoints, even if I don't agree with them. As St. Francis of Assisi said, I need to "seek to understand, rather than be understood." It means that I have to lighten up and not get so hung up on the petty stuff or beat myself up, especially when I make a mistake.

Bottom line, I need to be flexible, not only with my plans, but in my attitude and how I relate to myself, others, and the world around me.

In relation to solving problems or pursuing opportunities, I have learned that its prudent to have contingency plans and to be adaptable.

I have also learned to have a little more grace with myself. It's normal to have an occasional "bad-hair day." We all do.

Don't wallow in it. Instead, learn to ask and listen to what your emotions are saying to you. Look in the mirror. Talk to someone. Take a walk around the block or book a therapy session.

In private, take the time you need to sit with your feelings. Don't try to deny them, avoid them, or pretend they do not exist. No all-night pity parties. No playing the victim card. No blame, shame, guilt, or remorse.

Once you cool off, get back into the solution—back to work. Get back on your horse, grab the reins and boldly declare, "Giddy-up!"

As we accept and take responsibility for what we can control and let go of all that which is beyond our control, our confidence begins to soar. Things seem to flow easier. We don't feel so stressed out or get rattled so easily.

By letting go, we find the seat of our inner peace.

Gratitude is both a precursor and a prerequisite of happiness. Like happiness it is an emotional state we can choose and nurture or not. The beauty is that we get to choose. Nobody else has that power over us, unless we give it to them.

Again, it comes back to the Serenity Prayer:

"God, grant me the serenity to accept the things I cannot change, courage to change the things I can, and wisdom to know the difference."

The path of discovery is personal. Nobody can force us down a road we do not wish to explore. But through subtle but powerful shifts in our attitudes, actions, and words, we can take our eyes off ourselves to encourage others to seek their own path. To learn to trust their own light within. To be grateful for what we already have. To harness the courage each of us has but which we may have stashed in the attic along with our trunkful of dusty dreams.

Don't do that. Stop hiding it in the attic.

Instead, be bold and brave enough to embrace the power you already possess within and find the guts to take the next step in the direction of your dreams.

If you want exponential growth, extend an empathetic hand or warm embrace to someone who needs it. And most importantly, *forgive* and practice the subtle art of not being an asshole.

It really is that simple.

Don't complicate it.

Chapter 15: Generosity and The Joy of Giving

"You give but little when you give of your possessions.
It is when you give of yourself that you truly give."
Kahlil Gibran

I have been given one of the greatest gifts ever—a second chance at life. But this gift has a few strings. The twelfth step of recovery says this "Having had a spiritual awakening as the result of these steps, we tried to carry this message to alcoholics, and to practice these principles in all our affairs."

Sharing my experience strength and hope of living a sober life for more than thirty-eight years is an incredible responsibility and honor. I do it joyfully, not for fame or fortune, but because the hard-earned wisdom of dealing with life's perpetual ups and downs are gifts that I can share not only with those who suffer from addiction but who are suffering from lack of focus, fear, persistent anger or resentment, and a host of other "lifey" problems I have had to navigate just like all of us. The difference is that I have a fiduciary responsibility to share what I've learned as a condition of maintaining my sobriety.

This book and many others that I've written and will write, are simple gestures of giving back to a world that has given me more than I could have ever hoped or asked for.

I've known the highs and lows of a thousand and one extremes. I've also fought them and denied them only to discover that the pain of avoidance and resistance was far greater than learning to surrender and let go.

In that surrender I found hope.

This book is the crux of what I know as embracing the space between extremes. This is what has worked for and millions of others around the world. This book is a prelude to an even greater work than may take the rest of my lifetime to write, but if it is meant to be shared, it too will shed another beam of light onto a path toward peace. As Ram Dass says, **"We're all just leading each other home."**

For now, I will keep growing and learning and crossing off one struggle after another until my final breath. After all, what else is life but a series of lessons to be learned? And the real good ones, like the dream I had that inspired my memoir, cry out so loud that they beg to be heard. When they do, we must ask ourselves, *am I willing to listen? Are we brave enough to follow the prompts of our heart calling?*

Chapter 16: Full Circle—Every End is a New Beginning

"If you argue for your limitations, you get to keep them."
Unknown

By now you should be well equipped with the knowledge to focus your attention away from the magnetic pull of the extremes and find your balance point in between. Hopefully, too, you have a firmer grasp on the courage necessary to be more vulnerable and honest and to stop buying into the limits you place on yourself or allow others to place on your worth or ability.

It is my hope that I planted some seeds of kindness in your life; seeds of personal responsibility and a willingness to not be so myopic or narrow minded in your personal, professional, or political pursuits. That as a leader you will lean closer to what St. Francis taught: *to understand rather than be understood, to love rather than be loved...*

The paths you choose will determine the blueprints for each stage

of your life.

There is no perfect plan, only choices and decisions. We are all here to learn from each other and to pass on to the next generation some of the experiences we have gained. This is the foundation of all progress and the path to enlightenment and less suffering.

When we reframe and refocus our experiences and attitudes toward what we can do now we become alive. When we teach the earned wisdom to others, the whole world benefits.

However, when we wallow in the blame, or shame, or guilt of past mistakes we inevitably allow them to hold hostage our peace.

The paths you choose will determine the blueprints for each stage of your life.

So, too, are the countless hours you waste worrying about what could be, should be, or might never happen.

Worry is the Great Thief of Happiness

When we worry, we rob ourselves of the potential joys of hugging our kids or watching them score their first run, goal, or basket in the sport of life because we were worried that the other kids weren't being team players.

As adults, we too must be team players—at home, at work, and in the multitude of relationships we create and nurture. Nobody wants to belong to a group of tyrants. So, expand your circle, invite others in. As you do, you will become a more rounded and emotionally mature human capable of leading far more people than if you only rely on your own opinions or ideas.

Life is a collaboration. We are all connected, whether we admit it or not.

We're not meant to be live on a deserted island. Tom Hanks did that in *Castaway*, and it was awful. Similarly, there are no 100% self-made people. That's a myth that causes a host of many other problems not relevant for this book.

Self-awareness is a nice buzzword but how many really strive to know themselves better? To grow and mature as a species we must also take some time to know ourselves better, paying close attention to our personal and professional relationships.

As we close, here are a few reminders and one final story to ponder as you learn to embrace the space between your own extremes.

To me, life is not a winner take all proposition as some would have us believe. I am a firm believer of personal growth, starting with ourselves, and creating a vision that one day we will all learn to love and accept each other as we are.

Perhaps that's a pipe-dream or fairy tale.

Perhaps not.

Regardless, it's up to us to decide what is important and where to invest our time, talent, and energy. If we maintain a healthy perspective and attitude, life can be pretty freaking amazing.

I will not stop trying to add value to the lives of those I meet until my final breath. I will continue to write books and share inspirational stories that challenge us to examine our roles, responsibilities, and relationships in a healthier manner. Stories that encourage us to be better humans, to grow, and to *share what we learn with those willing to listen and hungry for positive change.*

Three Important Reminders:

- *Love* as if there is no tomorrow
- *Learn* as if your life depends on it
- *Dare* to practice something new and take a chance on *you, now*

Lastly, here's a story I've heard several times in several variations but it never loses its impact. May it linger on your heart long after our time together and help guide you as you begin the next phase of your life.

A Boy, a Dad, and a Map of the World

An executive is busy working in his home office when his six-year-old son comes in and starts asking him to play. After much persistence followed by much frustration, the exec pulls out a magazine and opens it to a large fold-out map of the world. Pulling out the map, he cuts it into hundreds of tiny pieces and gives them to his son. "Here, Son, after you put together this map of the world, then I'll play with you."

Knowing that a six-year-old has no idea what a map of the world looks like, he assumed that this task should keep his son busy for at least a couple hours.

But ten minutes later his son came back into the office and said, "All done, Daddy." The executive thought his son was exaggerating, but upon going into the living room, the entire map was perfectly assembled. "Son, how on earth did you figure out how to do this so quickly?"

"It was easy, Daddy." The boy began turning over the pieces one at a time, and as he did, his father saw that on the other side of the world map was a photograph of a man. **"You see, Daddy. When you put the man together the whole world falls into place."**

I hope that you take something valuable from our time together and more importantly, that you practice and share what you learn.

More will be revealed. Life is like that as long as we remain teachable.

Until we meet again, please don't forget to take time to chill. And always remember to embrace the space between extremes.

Onward, together.

Love,
Shawn

Many Hands...

All meaningful endeavors in life are collaborations. Writing and publishing a book are no exception. Up front, I want to thank my talented author wife, Crissi, who is not only my editor, but also formatter, proofreader, cover designer, and #1 cheerleader. I value your suggestions and love the title you came up with for this book. *Chill* is so fitting on so many levels.

To David O' Connor and Dale Godfrey, who, over several deep conversations, planted the seeds in my heart about the importance of relationships. I hope you are both smiling from heaven at this work you inspired through me.

To my late sponsor, Bobby B., thank you for never giving up on me and teaching me what emotional sobriety is all about.

To my mom and dad and other extended family who helped shaped my more encompassing perspectives about spirituality. Thank you for my crazy, middle-class, hippie upbringing!

To all who know me and love me and support me as I continue to write tough, heartfelt stuff for one sole purpose: to leave this world a little bit better than when I came into it.

May we all find the courage to embrace the spaces between our extremes. May we all begin to place a higher value and priority on this one transformational principle: Chill.

Other Books By Shawn Langwell:

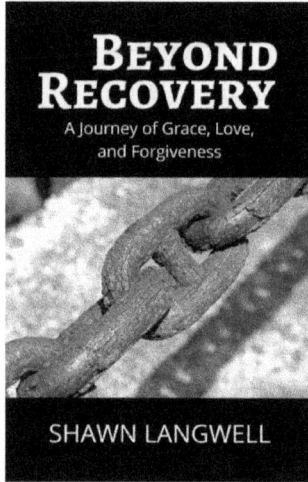

Beyond Recovery: An honest inspirational memoir about overcoming the pain of addiction and alcoholism, resentment, anger, fear, and low self-esteem, and what it took to find sobriety that lasts.

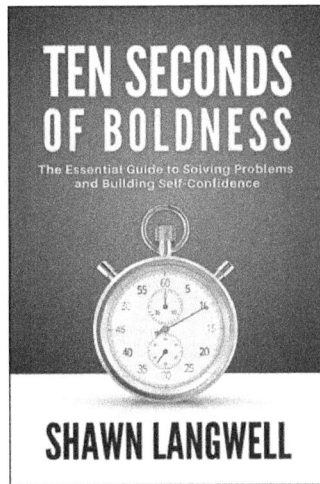

TEN SECONDS OF BOLDNESS
The Essential Guide to Solving Problems and Building Self-Confidence
SHAWN LANGWELL

Ten Seconds of Boldness: An inspirational, motivational, and practical self-help guide to stop overthinking, improve self-confidence, and accomplish your personal and professional goals.

Ten Seconds of Boldness outlines a simple yet transformational five-step method to move you from where you are to where you want to be in a way that is purposeful, meaningful, and lasting. Through personal experience and insights from influential leaders across the nation, Shawn Langwell will help you uncover the courage you need to overcome common roadblocks to success such as ***imposter syndrome, fear of failure, fear of success, overthinking, procrastination, and much more.***

TEN SECONDS OF BOLDNESS

Workbook

A simple yet transformational guide to move you from where you are to where you want to be

SHAWN LANGWELL

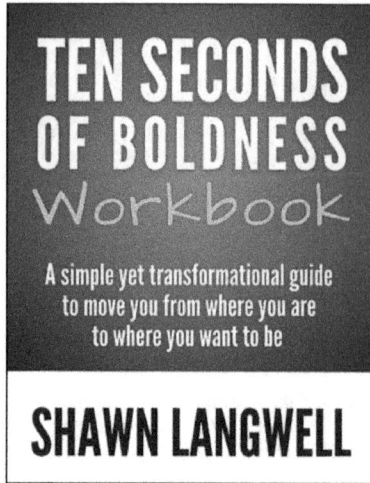

Ten Seconds of Boldness Workbook: This practical self-improvement workbook is for those who want a little encouragement, inspiration, and guidance to become bolder and more self-confident.

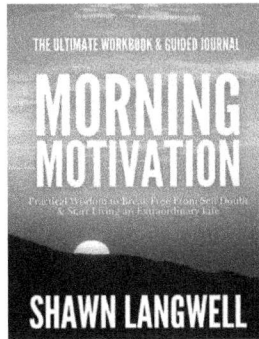

Morning Motivation is a great way to start your day with an attitude of gratitude and give you the tools you need to stop the steady din of self-doubt and gain the confidence you want so you can feel more alive.

If you're ready to start living a happier, more productive, meaningful, and fulfilling life, then this book is for you.

Speaking, Consulting, or Coaching Requests:

If you or your business are blocked, stagnating, or not reaching your full potential and could use a little inspiration, encouragement, and insight to help you resolve your growth and communication problems, please contact Shawn. His simple five-step approach to solving problems offers a more personalized, creative, and effective strategy than you currently may have.

Email: Shawnlangwellwriter@gmail.com

www.shawnlangwell.com

About the author:

Shawn Langwell is a leader, author, speaker, coach, and award-winning salesperson for the Bay Area News Group, and past salesperson and employee of the year for the New York Times Regional Media Group. He has over three decades of sales experience and thirty-eight plus years of continuous sobriety. In recovery, he has shared his personal story to thousands of people in more than twenty countries around the world.

He is the past president of Toast of Petaluma, and the past president of Redwood Writers, a branch of the California Writers Club, the largest writing club in California. He has written five inspirational books and is the host of the *Dare to Be Great. Dare to Be You Podcast.*

His personal mission is to add value to people and businesses everywhere. More specifically, to encourage, inspire, and help people become brave and confident enough to believe they can accomplish their dreams and goals.

Shawn lives in Northern California with his wife Crissi and Maine Coon cat Cleo.

You can find Shawn at shawnlangwell.com.

Email him at shawnlangwellwriter@gmail.com.

www.ingramcontent.com/pod-product-compliance
Lightning Source LLC
Chambersburg PA
CBHW060226030426
42335CB00014B/1346